D1329981

THE
TRANSPERSONAL
ACTOR

Reinterpreting Stanislavski

NED MANDERINO

Manderino Books
Los Angeles

The author wishes to express his gratitude to Anita Colby and Mary Hardy for their expert editorial assistance in the preparation of this book. And, of course, many thanks to "Chip" DuBose for his expert computer knowledge.

THE TRANSPERSONAL ACTOR:
Reinterpreting Stanislavski.

ISBN: 0-9601194-5-0
Library of Congress Catalog Number: 89-90782

Portions of this book previously published in **ALL ABOUT METHOD ACTING** © 1985 by Ned Manderino.

Manuscript Publication Design: Words & Deeds, Inc.
Printed by Edwards Brothers, Inc.
Computer Services by EWD Systems.

ACKNOWLEDGMENT

This book is dedicated to my "co-explorers," past and present. I am particularly grateful for their vision in sharing with me the untapped potential of the Stanislavski System. A prime selection of their imaginative exercise choices are contained throughout the book.

Contents

Part II The Transpersonal Actor

EXERCISE ABBREVIATIONS

Ch. Imp.—Channeling Impulse
        OA—Original Area
        PDA—Predetermined Area
Sp. Obj.—Spatial Objects
OSO—Outer Spatial Objects
IMO—Inner Moving Object
PSO—Projected Spatial Object
P&P—Physiological & Psychological Functioning

Foreword

This book is an outgrowth of *All About Method Acting*, a guide which contains the main principles of the Stanislavski System taught in America since the early 1920's, first by Russian immigrants and then by their American disciples.

All About Method Acting synthesizes all I had learned and absorbed from various teachers of the System during a period of 15 years. It was an important period in my life. In addition to having the opportunity to study with some of the major Stanislavski disciples in America, I had the good fortune to take part in numerous social occasions with them and to be on the periphery of their domestic lives. This unique opportunity provided first-hand observations which deepened my acquaintance with the evolution of the System in America.

This book examines my contribution to the evolution of the Stanislavski System. The Introduction provides a thumbnail sketch of my research into the divergent biographical material on Stanislavski. The first part deals with various forces that underpinned my reinterpretation of Stanislavski and led to my departure from my own teachers' approaches to the training of actors. The second, and most important section, outlines the transpersonal exercises with which I have experimented over the last 20 years. They have given actors the means to more fully refine their acting instruments.

This revised edition of *The Transpersonal Actor* offers a group of advanced exercises for the actor who has had solid training in the basic Stanislavski System. A discussion of the practical results I have observed actors attain in my workshop is included in the explanation of most of the new exercises. After twenty years of teaching, I am fully aware of how the System's basic sensory exercises and the use of actions have helped actors I have trained. However, I feel compelled to share the exercises contained in this book because they have been of supreme value in uncovering and solving problems that still remain in the instrument, even after extensive training in sensorial work and the use of actions.

The purpose of the transpersonal exercises is to open your instrument so that you can go beyond its present potential. Art endows humankind with immortal accomplishments. It does so by constantly traveling into new frontiers, often advancing ahead of the rest of civilization. So, I hope that the exercises will take you into new frontiers which will give you a new vision of acting as you refine the artistic material with which you experiment—yourself.

Author's Note

After much reflection, I have chosen not to refer to the major American Stanislavski disciples by name. I hope that this does not seem oblique to you and that you will understand my personal desire not to add to the considerable amount of material already published which has mentioned their names in an unflattering manner. I am aware of their contribution and grateful for the close relationships I was fortunate to have had with some of them.

INTRODUCTION

Introduction

Rereading Constantin Stanislavski's autobiography, *My Life in Art*, gave me the incentive to rewrite the 1976 edition of this book. In 1985, I believed the publication of *All About Method Acting* would prompt me to write its sequel. But that did not occur; I felt a lack of inspiration as I attempted to find a way to write a revision which would contain a sufficiently different viewpoint. I was seeking a framework in which to discuss my contribution to the development of the Stanislavski System. I needed a force that would propel me along the path of a more personal documentation of my beliefs. *My Life in Art* provided the force and the path.

One passage had particular significance for me. In 1906, sitting on a bench overlooking the Baltic Sea in Finland, Stanislavski ruminated over his inadequacies as an actor and concluded that the entrance into a role had to be personal and spiritual. He kept refining this concept for the remainder of his life. The passage inspired me to put my personal beliefs into this edition. The essence of Stanislavski's concept of a role dwells in the transpersonal philosophy which I have found reflected in all forms of the human potential movement that has continued to burgeon since the last edition of this book was published in 1976.

I was also deeply stirred by the spiritual content of Stanislavski's autobiography. I can recall no other theatre autobiography so immersed in spirituality and conviction about the existence of a Supreme Being. I was aware that such an interpretation of the Stanislavski System might meet with opposition, but it was necessary for me to proceed. I found the courage to do so while examining the vicissitudes of Stanislavski's life. His colleagues constantly attacked him; he fought Czarist censorship and Soviet bureaucracy; he was afraid that his first technique book, *An Actor Prepares* (still considered the bible for beginning actors of the System), would be attacked.

Rereading *My Life in Art* was the beginning of several months of extensive biographical research on Stanislavski. It was disconcerting to discover that one year after *My Life in Art* appeared, Stanislavski had rewritten it because he thought the first edition to be "naive." The two editions, the first in English and the second in Russian, were remarkably dissimilar. My initial reaction was that the Russian edition had been rewritten by someone else. Deeper research uncovered the reasons for the dissimilarity between the two editions.

Stanislavski resented politics entering his theatre. Though he was not a political person, I can only speculate that some of the revisions and additions in the second and subsequent editions were influenced by the political atmosphere of the Soviet Union during the first third of the century.

Stanislavski wrote most of the first edition during his two tours in America while Lenin was still the leader of Russia. Though Lenin proclaimed that art should serve state ideology, artists continued to enjoy a great degree of creative freedom during his lifetime. Similarly, Soviet policy regarding atheism was not as strictly enforced under Lenin as it would be later under Stalin. As soon as Stanislavski returned to Russia from America, he was under pressure to rewrite his autobiography. His System was under attack by the increasingly powerful avant-garde artists who considered his System a theatre art form that was too traditional, moribund and pedagogic. He also had to contend with the great change that the political atmosphere had undergone. Lenin had just died; Stalin and Trotsky were engaged in a power struggle. With the assistance of his long-time literary advisor, Liubov Gurevich, he set about the task of defending the System from attacks spurred by artistic, political, or religious differences. Though the spirit of the Russian revolution encouraged experimentation in the arts, by 1934 a policy of censorship was handed down in favor of socialist realism. Storm warnings were apparent in 1932 when Stalin prohibited literary forms that did not conform with socialist realism. When Stalin officially systematized socialist realism in 1934, the Moscow Art Theatre became the sole representative of socialist realism in theatre art.

The first and all subsequent editions of *My Life in Art* contain a chapter about the avant-garde movement. While Stanislavski disagreed with the movement's tenets in significant respects, he was enthusiastic about its innovative aspects and attempted to understand them. He acknowledged the movement's rightful place in the natural evolution of art, but advocated patience. He envisioned a time when his style of theatre might fuse with certain elements of the avant-garde style.

Although the avant-garde movement achieved significant breakthroughs in all the arts, we can only concentrate here on the movement's effect on the Stanislavski System. The years from 1917 to 1922 hold a supreme place in Russian theatre because artists were given free reign to develop a proletarian theatre which reflected a new time in Russian history. Directors and scene designers collaborated on developing a theatrical form of Constructivism and traditional theatre scenery gave way to kinetic and mechanical forms which created a potent three-dimensional use of space. As much as Stalin attempted to suppress the Constructivism of the avant-garde, it never truly disappeared. Today, Constructivism remains a vital force in Russian theatre and influences major theatre visionaries throughout the world.

In the first version of his autobiography, Stanislavski wrote that the strong approval given to avant-garde theatre artists made him feel like a conservative; in the Russian version he considers himself a Rightist. He was aware that the new political tide in Russia had no regard for conservatives and wanted citizens who would attend to the realities of everyday life. Stanislavski certainly was not conservative in his desire to fuse the new in art with the soul of the actor. His main objection to the avant-garde artists in the theatre was that they fostered an external style of acting. He found acting in the proletarian theatre to be soulless—a major problem for a man who believed that the soul of the actor is the most important component in theatre.

As early as 1905, he supported Vsevolod Meierhold in an experiment to create a new and mystical artistic form in the theatre similar to the forms that were developing in painting and music. Their move away from realism was a failure. Stanislavski returned to the realism of his still young System but believed throughout his life that Meierhold had found ways of reaching for the new in theatre art. Many years later, this common interest in breaking away from stale traditions would bring them together again.

The first edition of *My Life in Art* was written during some of the most exhilarating days of Stanislavski's life. In spite of a punishing performance schedule during his two American tours and a tight timeline from his publisher, Stanislavski was undeniably happy during this period. After his New York opening in 1923, he wrote both his wife and his colleagues that the Moscow Art Theatre had the greatest success it had ever experienced. In the first edition of his autobiography, he expressed his love for the American people and their curiosity for anything new. Artistically, he was very fulfilled by the praise and honor that American artists showered upon him and his company. He took great joy in American opera productions, which he felt were better than any in Europe and pronounced American symphony orchestras to be brilliant.

His delight in his American tour is not mentioned in the Russian edition. His two years in America are given one nondescript sentence. The second edition takes pains to acknowledge, apologetically, comrades that he did not emphasize or even mention in the first edition. Concurrently, it focuses less intently on certain other comrades who seemed very close to his heart in the first edition.

Meierhold, for example, with whom Stanislavski felt a spiritual kinship, is given only minor attention. The fact that Meierhold has no entry at all in the index of the Russian edition, may reflect his position as a lifetime enemy of socialist realism. It must have pained Stanislavski to minimize Meierhold's artistic importance in light of their joint effort to infuse the System with the new spirit in Russian arts. In spite of their differences (Meierhold denied the emphasis on psychological realities in the Moscow Art Theatre), they collaborated in a friendly manner in their search for innovation.

As his biographers have pointed out, the second edition is more of an atonement than a narrative of Stanislavski's life. In his final years, during a period of intense loneliness, Stanislavski again turned to Meierhold—the one remaining colleague with whom he felt a closeness. In the year before his death, Stanislavski returned to his first career interest—opera. He again worked with Meierhold in the hope that they could achieve something new. By this time, Stanislavski regarded Meierhold as heir to his System. With full knowledge of the Soviet government's hatred of Meierhold, Stanislavski permitted him to occupy the director's chair at the *Rigoletto* rehearsals. Perhaps Stanislavski could sense his own imminent death and saw his reconciliation with Meierhold as his final effort to work with a theatrical form which would reflect the modern spirit in art. His willingness to collaborate with Meierhold gave evidence of Stanislavski's artistic courage, as well as his refusal to tolerate the attempts of clumsy political bureaucrats to interfere with artists or the evolution of art in any form.

For a short time, the Soviet government permitted Meierhold to take Stanislavski's place at the Moscow Art Theatre after Stanislavski's death. Within one year, however, Meierhold's doom was sealed. At the 1939 All-Union Convention for Theatre Directors, Meierhold gave a fiery speech in which he proclaimed that socialist realism and art were incompatible. Shortly thereafter, he was arrested and accused of being a German spy. Undoubtedly, the efforts of German and Russian artists to join forces in the formation of a strong avant-garde movement gave the government the pretext it needed for accusations against Meierhold and his subsequent arrest. His ultimate fate is uncertain. Some say he was tortured and murdered in a Moscow prison, others say he committed suicide in a concentration camp, and still others believe he just disappeared. But everyone knew the facts of his wife's barbarous assassination.

In addition to changes in political content, the Russian edition of *My Life in Art* is stripped of the numerous religious references that appeared in the English edition. References to God the Father and Christ the Lord, and the dutiful observance of Easter, Lent, and other religious holidays are all omitted in the Russian edition. In the English version, Stanislavski speaks of an actor's talent as a gift from God and an actor's inspiration as bequeathed by Apollo. In the Russian edition, only Apollo is mentioned.

Even though Stanislavski may not have attended church with great regularity in his adult years, he thought religion important enough to have a religious ceremony before the first 1898 rehearsal of the Moscow Art Theatre. The final line which he wrote in the English version is a prayer requesting assistance in his work.

Many have discovered rich biographical information in the English edition. Stanislavski, however, regretted that he did not give more attention to the creative part of his System. But we have long had his technique books to complete whatever he felt was omitted.

As a Stanislavski researcher, I favor the joy and casual

feeling of the English edition. It has the free-flowing spontaneity of *An Actor Prepares*. The Russian edition, in compari-
son, is rather arid in tone. Because it apologizes for nothing
and deals so openly with questions of spirituality, the first
edition of *My Life in Art* continues to strike the more respon-
sive chord in me.

PART I

REINTERPRETING STANISLAVSKI

Part I
Reinterpreting Stanislavski

FROM NAZIMOVA TO BRANDO

The great actress, Alla Nazimova, was Stanislavski's first illustrious student to perform in America. She played secondary roles in the early years of the Moscow Art Theatre, but by 1904 she was engaged as a leading lady in St. Petersburg. She created more than two hundred roles in Russian theatres. In 1905, she became a notable actress in America, first performing in her native tongue in a dilapidated Russian theatre on New York's Lower East Side. Critics praised the productions in which she appeared, impressed by their realism and psychological depth; one said that the performances were "intensely modern and revolutionary." In 1906, she made her English-speaking debut in a production of Ibsen's *Hedda Gabler*. The play had a far greater success in America than at the Moscow Art Theatre, where it suffered a quick demise even though Stanislavski's performance in it was considered to be of genius stature. Nazimova continued to give memorable performances of powerful sensitivity for over thirty years, specializing in Ibsen, but also performing Chekhov and Shaw. Eugene O'Neill was impressed by her Ibsen performances and offered her a demanding role in his monumental drama, *Mourning Becomes Electra*. She last appeared on Broadway in 1939, starring in *The Mother* with Montgomery Clift. Her tropical estate in Hollywood later became a hotel known as The Garden of Allah, the legendary scene of sensuality, parties, pranks, and a cavalcade of every conceivable human drama— marriage, divorce, suicide, murder, and robbery. It was an internationally known playground that attracted an impressive roster of intellectuals and celebrated performers.

Nazimova's distinguished performances gave America its first glimpse of a high-caliber star trained in the Stanislavski System. Perhaps because her arrival in America preceded that of other major Stanislavski-trained actors by decades, she is rarely linked to the Stanislavski System. Actors more often associated with the System include Maria Ouspenskaya, a pioneer teacher and actress of the System in America who never reached Nazimova's star stature; John Garfield and Franchot Tone, who established themselves as the first Americans to be influenced by the System; and, forty-two years after Nazimova's arrival in America, Marlon Brando, who solidified the System's American contribution to 20th Century acting.

STANISLAVSKI VISITS AMERICA

In 1923, Constantin Stanislavski and a contingent from the Moscow Art Theatre first toured America, and audiences saw why the theatre had become known for a style of spiritual realism. Stanislavski was rapturous over the New York opening. During the American tour, he and his actors were received, though with a perceivable lack of graciousness, by President Calvin Coolidge, becoming the first Soviet citizens to have a reception at the White House. While touring America, Stanislavski began to write his autobiography, *My Life in Art*. He completed the bulk of the work during his two American tours in 1923 and 1924, apparently to meet a contractual agreement with his American publisher who released the first edition in 1924.

Two members of the Moscow Art Theatre, Richard Boleslavsky and the aforementioned Ouspenskaya, remained in America and began the American Laboratory Theatre. Due largely to their work, the United States became the first foreign country to embrace the Russian-born System. From among their hundreds of students came the major American disciples of the System.

The quarrelsome tide concerning the proper use of the System in America might not have developed if Stanislavski had been well enough to accept the American Laboratory Theatre's invitation in 1928 to teach for eight months. He had received an earlier invitation in 1924 to open his own studio in New York. If he had accepted either of these invitations, Stanislavski could have set the American use of his System on course. Instead, his American disciples visited Stanislavski in Paris and Moscow and returned with acrimoniously divergent concepts of the System.

Although it is one hundred years old, the System has not evolved in America in accordance with the vision of inevitable exploration and growth that Stanislavski foretold in his autobiography. In *My Life in Art*, Stanislavski expresses his desire that others further his discoveries to reach a higher consciousness. This requires taking leave of some of his more well-known theories in order to go beyond them. Without a doubt, Stanislavski regarded his System as evolutionary. My personal viewpoint is that the System has, unfortunately, been trapped in the creative think tank of the 1930's. By 1930, most of Stanislavski's basic ideas had taken hold in America. Since then, these basic theories have been refined and clarified, but they have rarely been explored in ways which have led to the evolutionary process desired by Stanislavski. He had cautioned Joshua Logan in 1931 that Americans should find their own way into his System because of the differences between the Russian and American societies. He advised Logan that Americans should experiment with his System and avoid being doctrinaire. Clearly, a vital part of Stanislavski's message concerning the art of acting has been largely overlooked.

Throughout his life Stanislavski regarded the nature of acting energy as spiritual. He believed the soul to be of prime importance in an actor's ability to balance the physical and the spiritual. At the American Laboratory Theatre, Boleslavsky referred to the soul when discussing the inner work of the actor. Subsequently, others with a more scientific bent referred to the nervous system and the word "soul" disappeared from American discussions of the System. Today, there is no agreement concerning the spiritual component of the System.

STYLE AND THE SYSTEM

Laurence Olivier, whom many revere as this century's greatest actor, said that Stanislavski was the most important acting teacher of the 20th Century. While acknowledging the influence that Stanislavski had in England in 1920, Olivier has been somewhat disturbed by what Stanislavski's disciples in America have done with the System. Many of his fellow English actors, and even some American actors, feel that the Stanislavski practitioners in America have over-emphasized truth and naturalism.

Attempts to develop an American answer to the historical style displayed by the great theatre companies of England and other European nations was a complete failure. The artists who were given the task of developing a style with which American actors could perform the world's greatest classics were mostly disciples of the System, and they freely admit their lack of success. Some critics fault the System for not solving the problem of historical style by integrating its passion for inner conviction with the technical virtuosity needed for the compelling emotional peaks of historical dramas. I feel that the System has failed to achieve credible style values because it has not been sufficiently developed in a way that encompasses Stanislavski's entire philosophy. His lifelong desire was for the System to be successfully applied to the classics and not limited to plays depicting the raw emotions of everyday life.

INCORPORATING STANISLAVSKI'S HUMANISTIC VISION

As I have expressed in previous editions of this book, I feel that long ago the Stanislavski System should have been used as a springboard into new areas of consciousness. Instead, the central core of teaching the System in America today remains the same sensory and emotional memory exercises that were taught by Boleslavsky at the American Laboratory Theatre in the 1920's. The relentless pursuit of these exercises has bogged down the System's creative potential. The evolution of this book through three editions has been my attempt to give Stanislavski a more progressive essence by constantly expanding his theories. From the results I have seen in teaching actors for the past 20 years, I have concluded that the conventionalities present in various versions of the System have not provided the spiritual development that Stanislavski's humanistic vision considered essential.

As an artist and social theorist, Leo Tolstoy exerted a significant influence on Stanislavski's professional and spiritual growth. Both men believed the theatre to be a more effective forum for the masses than either church or school and both felt that a work of art should impart moral lessons. Tolstoy, a believer in non-violence and passive resistance before either Gandhi or King, devoted many years of his life to spiritual self-purification. His play, *The Fruits of Enlightenment*, successfully established Stanislavski as a theatre director. There can be little doubt that Stanislavski, like his closest friend the multi-talented artist Leopold Sulerjitsky, embraced the spiritual meaning in Tolstoy's philosophy. Stanislavski also shunned the non-spiritual nature of Marxist doctrine. He disdained directing or producing Soviet plays and believed the Moscow Art Theatre contributed to society by presenting the classics.

While Tolstoy strove for natural simplicity in his life and art, Stanislavski attempted to reach ever higher levels of spiritual consciousness. He attempted to lead his actors into spiritual realms in both their acting endeavors and in their personal lives. His philosophy espoused the development of "a new actor in the new life." From the first, his rebellion against vapidly external acting met with resistance from his fellow actors at the Moscow Art Theatre. He felt that the ascendancy of the art of acting to a spiritual level of consciousness required a new species of actor with a completely new technique. Each of the subsequent discoveries in his quest for an acting style of truthful behavior was considered by some to be merely his latest fad. Nevertheless, as a man committed to spiritual growth, he was not deterred from broadening his vision.

Few words capture the essence of Stanislavski's spiritual quest as well as "incarnation." He wanted the System to provide the means whereby an actor could embody the spirit or "incarnation" of a role and give it the most human form obtainable. When one finds the word in his book *Creating a Role*, "incarnation" refers to expressions of the face, use of voice and speech, gesture and movement. These basic elements fall short of creating the complete "incarnation" that Stanislavski envisioned. Segments of *Creating a Role* were drafted in 1916, with two further drafts written in the 1930's. In 1935, Stanislavski revealed to Norris Houghton that he was still seeking a solution to the problem of "incarnation." This remained his main unfulfilled desire.

Stanislavski met with opposition regarding his System particularly from Michael Chekhov, the most spiritually inclined of his colleagues. Chekhov believed in the use of the whole person in acting, finding Stanislavski's emphasis on emotional memory too limited. While some of Stanislavski's American disciples also disagreed concerning the use of emotional memory and emphasized physical actions instead, they also rejected Chekhov's vision of a spiritual consciousness as too mystical for the System. In spite of their disagreements, Stanislavski and Chekhov concurred on the need to nurture an actor's spiritual dimensions, even if from different viewpoints. The two remained friends. There is evidence that Chekhov might have become Stanislavski's heir if Stanislavski could have convinced Chekhov, who had emigrated due to the political climate, to return to Russia.

Spirituality, according to the best of consciousness philosophies, means going beyond oneself in order to reach one's fullest potential. Historically, artists have always been intrigued by spiritual elements, particularly those related to higher states of consciousness. Numerous creative people follow such paths in their natural stride. Sometimes, these people are a little ahead of their time. The course of civilization determines whether others will catch up sufficiently to share their vision. No one today, however, can fail to be aware of the advent of the enormous changes long predicted by visionaries. The best of today's new spirit is focusing on conserving the planet. This necessitates a shift of consciousness towards a spiritual level as more and more we cherish the belief that we are on this earth as co-creators in a universal spirit, and, by fulfilling certain obligations, we improve upon our planet. George Gurdjieff, a pioneer in consciousness philosophy, believed that if we are unable to care for a plant or animal, we ultimately relinquish responsibility for each other and our planet's natural resources. The new level of consciousness presently flowering on our struggling planet has taken many millennia to arrive. Stanislavski singled out the lack of spiritual content as the catalyst for humankind's destructiveness towards nature. He emphasized that his System was based on observations of both human beings and nature.

CONSCIOUSNESS LEVELS

Stanislavski envisioned an acting technique that could capture the essence of those changes in consciousness that involve spiritual capacities. Resting in a sanitarium near Moscow in 1935, several years before his death, he told a group of visitors that thoroughly trained actors can forget their technique training and abandon themselves to what he described as the fourth story of consciousness. Again, as he had so many times before, he spoke of the actor of the future whose art would rest on inspirational intuition. The actor's instrument would be trained in such a way that the mechanics of technique need not be dwelled upon. Stanislavski's observations of the virtuoso effortlessness of the Italian actors Rossi, Salvini and Zacconi inspired this belief.

Some of Stanislavski's major American disciples, living on the plane of consciousness of their time, may have sincerely believed that they had succeeded in reaching the fourth story. Nonetheless, today's fourth story houses a very different type of consciousness than that attainable with sensory technique exercises, emotional memory, or the use of physical actions.

The intention of the systematic training program I have developed is that the actor form a different kind of artistic consciousness so that in his/her professional work the results of technique exercises are retained even when the techniques themselves are not consciously employed. A few of the various technique exercises that I have developed since the previous editions of this book are included herein. They are an outgrowth of my continuing endeavor to develop a technique that is suited for any style required of the actor.

THE AMERICAN DISCIPLES

Stanislavski was adamant about others carrying on his work. He told his favorite pupil, Eugene Vaghtangov (a mystic who envisioned the theatre as a monastery) that he taught the System with a greater excellence. There is little of Stanislavski's willingness to pass on the torch to be found in the attitude of his early American disciples. It would be difficult to find a comment such as that made by Stanislavski to Vaghtangov among the recorded utterances of his American disciples, whose artistic and personal triumphs (and shortcomings) have already been described in numerous articles and books. They believed their accomplishments to be the final word on the development of the System, and some have not looked favorably upon any departure from their solutions. Each felt that he or she alone was entitled to be the sole Stanislavski heir, and none was willing to entertain a new perspective. The bitter infighting over who was the rightful interpreter of the System left little room for an openness to experiment with the System as Vakhtangov, Meierhold and Chekhov were doing in Russia, experiments which Stanislavski held in high esteem. Instead, the American disciples fought for recognition as the one who, single-handedly, had discovered the path to the heightened expressiveness which Stanislavski had searched for but never found.

Some have pointed out that one of the major failures of the American disciples was a lack of communication and sharing of ideas. What matters most among artists, even if they disagree, is that they share some kind of spiritual bond—as difficult as that may be in today's competitive atmosphere. Only in the sharing of ideas can art remain open to new ideas and realities. Stanislavski voiced this sentiment at his seventieth birthday celebration.

DISAGREEMENT AMONG THE DISCIPLES

Stanislavski's first technique book, *An Actor Prepares*, took 35 years of preparation. It was not published until 1936, when Stanislavski was 73 years old. He was haunted before the book's publication with memories of an earlier time when colleagues regarded his theories as trifling and unimportant. His later works contradict *An Actor Prepares* in significant ways.

Stanislavski was always growing and exploring new ideas and regularly questioned his own theories and beliefs. He was known to quibble with himself while leisurely exploring ideas. Perhaps this explains, in part, why as many as 300 rehearsals were sometimes held for his productions. Lengthy rehearsal periods gave him time to test the validity of his ideas through acting experiments he and his actors undertook. The development of theories often takes circuitous routes. Darwin worked on his theory for 20 years only to discover that another naturalist had arrived at the same theory while in a week-long state of delirium.

During the main stage of development, the System emphasized emotional memory, the magic "as if," the given circumstances which contained the use of physical actions and the ruling idea of a drama. Jean Benedetti in his excellent biography examines a summary of the System which Stanislavski prepared several weeks before his death. The summary includes the superobjective, actions, physical actions, images, inner monologue, improvisation, the given circumstances, inner and outer elements of a character, use of actual people for role models, energy, rhythm, tempo and the ruling idea. At the end of the Russian version of his autobiography, Stanislavski sums up his System by stating that it basically requires an actor to work on personal inner and outer values as well as the inner and outer values of a role. The ever-searching Stanislavski acknowledged that there were still unexplored areas and hoped that he could live longer for he felt that he had just begun his search.

While Stanislavski explored his System, his disciples were all independently working with it from different perspectives—emphasizing certain parts of the System and omitting others. This never annoyed him. He knew, for example, that Boleslavsky was teaching emotional memory to young American disciples, while he was giving attention to physical actions and objectives. He even gave his blessings to Boleslavsky to teach as he wished. Boleslavsky's lectures at the American Laboratory Theatre emphasized the use of dramatic actions, while in Russia Stanislavski was developing physical actions. Some of the early American disciples were drawn to the use of dramatic actions; others were drawn to emotional memory. After visiting Stanislavski, some disciples began to promulgate the use of physical actions over emotional memory. This division in the System was at the core of the disagreements which flared in the mid-30's. The disagreements, however, stemmed from more than the major controversy concerning emotional memory versus physical actions. A lack of tolerance for each disciple's tendency to work in his/her own way lay at the center of the disagreements.

However, the American disciples shared one important common interest, and that was to find a way of using the

System to bring truth into American acting. The one major omission of the disciples was Stanislavski's wish that his System be used for the classics. The productions of his American disciples were chosen to convey the social milieu of America in the 30's.

Stanislavski's interest in physical actions during his final years was based on his conviction that work with physical actions contained the stimulus needed to arrive at the truth of a role. This conviction sparked a division in the most vital and dynamic theatre group that America has ever known, a division which eventually led to the group's total collapse. One side felt that Stanislavski had gone back on himself by de-emphasizing emotional memory; the other side seized eagerly upon the use of physical actions. Stanislavski always regretted the great split he caused and believed both sides were justified. Perhaps, if he had been in a better state of health, Stanislavski might have taken measures to arrange an armistice between the warring factions and given them the much needed inspiration to cooperate while experimenting with his System. Without this intervention, the infighting became too severe to reconcile. The relationship between the American disciples contrasts sharply with that of Stanislavski and Nemirovich-Danchenko. As co-directors of the Moscow Art Theatre, they weathered a series of disagreements and reconciliations and gave birth to a theatre which still exists after nearly a century.

The quarrel over physical actions versus emotional memory was, in my opinion, somewhat futile. If Stanislavski had lived he would have continued with his customary disposal of some of his previous theories and physical actions might have been de-emphasized in the same way that he had de-emphasized emotional memory. At one point he quipped that an idiot must have developed the theory of emotional memory.

I have always attempted to give credence to all of Stanislavski's discoveries because I believe that they are all harbingers for his final unfulfilled goal of "a new actor in the new life." His ideas do not contradict one another but are simply products of his process of moving into new territories. He is not the first person in history who died without completely realizing a complex goal. Two years before his death, he was still dissatisfied and still searching for a means of helping the actor to reach creative truth. He castigated himself for not arriving at certain theories at a much earlier time in his life. At one of his last rehearsals, he expressed regret that he had not clarified many things. At his final rehearsal, he emphatically exclaimed that he did not want to die because he had just begun to find solutions. What were those solutions that he had just begun to find? It is possible that they were not the solutions over which his American disciples were quarreling. On his deathbed, his weak arms pantomimed leafing through the pages of a book, still in search of growth and self-knowledge.

As for his technique books in which many seek answers, he asserted that none of them could give an individual the golden key. Neither physical actions nor emotional memory exclusively contains the means to help an actor to develop the flexible kind of acting instrument that Stanislavski deemed necessary for the "incarnation" of a role. Physical actions, emotional memory, as if, objectives, given circumstances, etc., are all contributing elements to the "incarnation" of a role and all should be explored and practiced by a developing actor. Physical actions are important because they create the inner life of a character which is manifested externally. Much of the work with physical actions helps the actor give language to objects which surround a character and create behavior and activities which reveal the nature of the character. At the same time that the physical actions versus emotional memory quarrel was raging in America, Stanislavski was refining his exploration of the way moments in an actor's personal life relate to those in a character's.

Most serious actors pursue different approaches to the System and integrate various parts, making it difficult to tell which of the System's principles have had the greatest influence on them. An eclectic pursuit of the System follows the example of Stanislavski who became his own best teacher. However, such an endeavor requires that the actor search as diligently as Stanislavski in order to be transformed into an autonomous artist. Stanislavski became an autonomous artist by constantly questioning himself. He knew that there would never exist a single theory which could describe the entire process of an actor's art. Disagreements will persist. Your duty to yourself is to capture the spirit of the time in which you live and that is accomplished by fully utilizing and breaking with established theories to create innovative approaches.

Nearly every approach to acting in any country incorporates Stanislavski's principles of truth and honesty in an effort to avoid external and conventional acting. His theories have been turned inside out, resulting in many mutations. Most of the early American teachers of the System avoided the higher levels of consciousness that are inherent in his philosophy. Instead, they promulgated the isolated segments of Stanislavski's vision with which they were capable of establishing a connection. As Joseph Campbell believed, beneath higher consciousness lies lower levels of consciousness, and it is on a less developed level that I feel the American representation of the System has languished.

With their individualistic interpretations, the early American disciples became esteemed teachers with over-flowing classes. Often these classes in the ABC's of the System were more inspirational than practical. By failing to emphasize the importance of daily, rigorous practice—an ingredient of success recognized by young artists engaged in every other art form —the classes often resulted in the development of a hit-or-miss technique. Failure to recognize the evolutionary nature of the System and its integrative potential made it difficult for the American disciples to develop the System beyond its original boundaries. Einstein's basic relativity theory was only understood by two or three people in 1920. Today, it is taught to high school students, while unsolved parts of his visionary theory are the chief concern of the world's leading physicists. Unfortunately, the unsolved parts of Stanislavski's visionary theories were of little concern to his American disciples.

THE ACTOR'S NERVOUS SYSTEM— THEN AND NOW

The Boleslavsky exercises, which remain the central emphasis in certain Stanislavski schools of technique, were meaningful in the 1920's and 1930's for developing the sensitivity of an actor's nervous system. By sensitizing the nervous system, sensory training begins a process of trans-formation, but this beginning is not sufficient for today's actors. Just as medical science does not continue to treat a person with outdated methods when new means are available, the art of acting should not rely upon techniques which have not kept pace with the realities of the late 20th Century. Today, the actor's nervous system yearns for higher realities, not the experiences of a constrained acting instrument. Like athletes, who, with training, technique, and equipment, establish records considered impossible fifty years ago—only to be surpassed by a new champion at the next Olympic games—today's dedicated actor strives toward new challenges and higher goals.

We no longer live in the comparatively static world of the 1920's and 1930's, which was congenial to the use of sensory technique exercises. A cyclical succession of bewildering world events has changed everything. Today, we constantly receive new information about ourselves and the expanding world in which we live. The potential zeniths of a New Age create an obligation for the actor to explore greater heights in acting. The System must incorporate new technique exercises to enable the actor to respond to the stimuli present in his/her world. I believe that this is what Stanislavski envisioned when he spoke of "a new actor in the new life." By embracing a technique which involves the sensorium of the entire acting instrument, the actor can then feel that he/she is reflecting the realities of a new generation.

Stanislavski believed that each new generation is able to perceive with different eyes. The way in which he has been perceived by his founding American disciples no longer fits into the present scheme of realities, particularly with the rapid approach of the third millennium and its brimming promises of great discoveries for the benefit of humankind. The new century will require actors, as well as all others, to make innumerable paradigm shifts. Many feel that the survival of civilization requires a new species of humans. Stanislavski felt that a new species of actor with a completely new technique was needed to permit the art of acting to ascend to a spiritual level of consciousness.

Sensory awareness in the human experience has now given way to an expansion of the consciousness. Consciousness awareness exercises enable the individual to make contact with the higher creative energy centers of the spiritual part of our psyches. In his works, Stanislavski coined the word "superconscious" to allude to the state that an actor should strive toward. Today, Stanislavski's concept of the "superconscious" would be associated with Zen Buddhism or spiritual mysticism. The superconscious, for Stanislavski, began where the mundane aspects of life ended. The prevalence of this word in Stanislavski's books offers a clue to the importance he placed on spiritual awareness. He was also a man of great forgiveness. The day before his death he expressed concern for Nemirovich-Danchenko's health—a poignant expression of his concern for the man who had so severely criticized Stanislavski's acting in *The Village of Stepanchikovo*. Evidently, Nemirovich-Danchenko's criticism permanently wounded Stanislavski as he never undertook a new role for the final 20 years of his life.

EXPANDING THE SYSTEM

Once I was convinced that I had dissected all of the details of the human anatomy in every possible and imaginable way to create new behavioral changes, I believed I was ready to document my personal interpretation of the Stanislavski System in this revised edition. This work represents a refined understanding of the transpersonal exercises that appeared in the 1973 and 1976 editions. This understanding deepened as I witnessed my students experiencing a new System aesthetic. Since the 1976 edition, I have seen the transpersonal exercises validated more and more by the expanding awareness of consciousness in the world. For example, the Brain Exercise, through which I have seen actors achieve outstanding behavioral results, was considered unimportant and even destructive in 1973. Five years later, when an extremely popular book on the creative development and use of the brain was published, the Brain Exercise became less menacing. Innumerable "brain" books, seminars, and workshops later, I feel justified in having dismissed those early antagonistic responses to the Brain Exercise. Similarly, certain of my other exercises, which seemed abstract to some, gained increasing acceptance as their premises began to be supported and verified by expanding consciousness research.

My workshop for actors continues to serve as my laboratory. Students eagerly experiment with new exercises to gain additional acting tools. Each tool can be accepted or, if it does not suit an actor's particular creative chemistry, rejected. A creative artist has the prerogative to accept or reject—otherwise, what is the meaning of creativity? I have not subjected my students to the kind of Stanislavski training I received, during which an entire year might be devoted to one simplistic sensory exercise. No wonder this century's foremost American stage and film director said that the entire problem with the use of the System in America is that it has failed to get out hidden energies. No wonder Stanislavski himself implied that actors studying his System without expanding it would not be able to find its potency.

OUR ROLE IN THE EVOLUTION OF THE SYSTEM

Certain naturally gifted actors may only need the basics of the System to discover that their gift is already fully developed. For a far greater majority of actors, however, the narrow use of the System commits an injustice by creating inertia and failing to nurture their creative promise. If Stanislavski were alive today to observe prominent actors attaining career breakthroughs with a little help from his basic principles, he would undoubtedly offer numerous observations concerning his System.

Many times in his life, he found it difficult to articulate his beliefs. But, he believed that each of us has the ability to reach greater artistic heights by not relying completely on the System. He developed his System so that the actor could be truthful and logical in a character's situation. The need for truth and logic also applies to the development of a heightened artistic consciousness in our time and the seizure of our moment in the long evolution of the System.

After nearly one hundred years, it is imperative that Stanislavski's vision be imbued with a new kind of spiritual energy. This must happen, because there is no other way to boot the System into its third century. Conceived in the 19th Century, Stanislavski's System has evolved gradually throughout most of the 20th Century. It is time to start moving the System into present-day consciousness and toward the future consciousness of the 21st Century when the theatre should become more vigorous and dynamic than it has ever been if it is to capture the energy of the next millennium.

An experimental psychologist and professor at the Sorbonne by the name of Theodule Ribot wrote a book entitled

The Psychology of the Emotions. It was Ribot who gave Stanislavski the germ of the idea of emotional memory, the exercise which has caused so much controversy. Similarly and appropriately, Stanislavski's American disciples were influenced by the great thinkers of their time. In the 1930's, they read about Freud's road to the complex state of human thought and emotions in the subconscious, along with William James and C.G. Lange. But, in what way is the new generation educating itself? We currently have access to a much better education than Stanislavski. He found school dull and debilitating to his mind and could only find delight in circuses, theatre, ballet, operas and home theatrics. We can read and study the ideas of many fine minds. To mention just a few: Jung, Erickson, Horney, Perls, Reich, Ouspensky, Huxley, Reik, Laing, Rogers, Skinner, Allport, Gurdjieff, Fromm, Kris, Jaynes, Rank, Campbell, Lilly, Ram Dass, Auribindo, Herrigel, Capra, Grof, Tulku, Muktananda, and the innovative humanists, Assagioli and Maslow. The System, as Stanislavski envisioned it is open and receptive to all of the new knowledge of our time. All that Stanislavski's vision needs is our imaginative insight as to how to use new knowledge to give the System new meaning.

Actors must develop their vocal and physical stamina to play the demanding roles created by great playwrights of centuries ago, as well as of our own time. Otherwise, actors cannot possibly possess the kind of artistic longevity that is enjoyed by musicians, singers, and dancers. Throughout their hard and never-ending training they are always searching for new heights. They embrace the advice Stanislavski was given by the great actor Ernesto Rossi who told Stanislavski that the best teacher is oneself. That pivotal advice started Stanislavski on his search; by teaching himself, he began to formulate his System.

Stanislavski would certainly support our efforts to change the System. It is the only possible way for us to preserve it and take it to new creative frontiers. He would want us to honor the art of acting with a new consciousness so that the art can reach new heights.

MY LIFE IN ART

The first edition of *My Life in Art* contains all the clues needed to envision what Stanislavski might have eventually accomplished with his System.

I first read *My Life in Art* many years ago. During the final phase of long preparation for this new edition, I read it again. I quickly became aware that the kind of consciousness that led to my development of his System was validated in his autobiography. I experienced the same exaltation that Stanislavski felt when he read Luigi Riccaboni's 18th Century book, *Reflections on Recitation*, and found that Riccaboni's theories corroborated his own.

Rereading *My Life in Art* was like a blast of fresh air for me. I discovered levels of meaning with which I had not fully come to terms years before. His autobiography, more than his popular technique books, has many references to the spiritual in acting. By spiritual, Stanislavski did not necessarily imply matters of a theological nature, although the book mentions his dutiful observance of religious holidays and makes frequent references to God. Instead, his concept of the spiritual implied the growth and fulfillment of one's given potential. He mirrored the spiritual regeneration which occurred at the turn of the century in Russia and wanted actors to reject materialism in preference to spiritu-alism. His goal was to show the actor how to use the energy of spiritual dimensions to propel the acting instrument upward.

In *My Life in Art,* he refers to spiritual practice, spiritual apparatus, spiritual strength, spiritual juices, spiritual dis-cipline, spiritual technique, spiritual mood, spiritual prob-lems, spiritual progress, spiritual rays and spiritual influ-ence. To a lesser extent, his technique books also communi-cate his concern with the spiritual. Here he looks at the meanings of spiritual atmosphere, spiritual communica-tion, spiritual naturalism, spiritual life, spiritual wellsprings and spiritual nature. In his autobiography, he makes it clear that he considered the art of theatre to be spiritual. His concept of the spiritual, especially as expressed in the Eng-lish edition's final chapter, fits in easily with the current thinking of consciousness writers regarding holism, peak experiences and the recognition of human potential.

Despite the many changes he made during the develop-ment of his System, the spiritual goal was always present in his nature, figuring as prominently as physical actions, emotional memories, and sensorial feelings. The final chap-ter of the autobiography offers a good introduction to his personal and aesthetic concept of spirituality. I heartily recommend that it be read as a preamble to his technique books. In it, he mentions the need for the young generation of his time to find a "new life" to move forward from the catastrophic events that had occurred in the world since he first began to develop his System. I feel that his recognition of the new needs that arise with changing realities is related to my own beliefs that certain aspects of the System do not adequately serve the higher levels of consciousness in the "new life" of today's young generation of actors who face potentially even more catastrophic world events.

Some of the American disciples believed that Stanislavski never solved certain problems in the System and that they had done it for him. After years of study, research, and teaching, I must conclude that the one problem that Stanislavski never solved is how to develop techniques that lead to spiritual dimensions—an area into which the American Stanislavski pioneers rarely ventured and offered few insights.

A NEW GENERATION STAYS OFF TRACK

Unfortunately, the new generation of Stanislavski acting teachers has merely perpetuated the pioneers' beliefs with some minor modifications. Many of the new teachers have claimed their own territory by emphasizing certain aspects of what they learned from the pioneers. Some are orthodox practitioners of the use of the System, emphasizing the private moment, affective memory, sense memory, animal exercise, as if, inner monologue, etc. Some have developed their own exercises, most of which have their origin in traditional Stanislavski. Few offer the System the spiritual flesh for which it yearns.

Some of the new generation of teachers, following the path of their mentors, have become psychologists practicing without a license. Some of the original disciples promulgated the theory that acting problems are personal, psychological problems that must be removed before the acting instrument can be used effectively. In certain cases, they indulge in versions of the Freudian couch. As a teacher, I have never felt comfortable prying directly into a person's psyche. However, by emphasizing the use of a different action, at each session, in conjunction with sensory and/or transpersonal choices I indirectly promote self-examination. I have observed that most of my students are in tune with their personal hang-ups and sensitive enough to do their own head shrinking through the selection of appropriate actions. My workshop uses an array of imaginative improvisational situations, rather than primal screams or hot-seat interrogations. Actors' personal feelings and behavior are vented in the dramatic situation of an improvisation so that creative and personal growth occur simultaneously.

Only the spiritual aspect of Stanislavski's philosophy will permit the actor to explore the acting instrument to its very depths and furthest range. Although some of the new generation of acting teachers proclaim that their new exercises and techniques—though based almost exclusively on traditional, orthodox Stanislavski—will become the acting methods of the future, I find their solutions far from desirable for the spiritual interests of many young actors. Their methods may get the juices flowing for some outstanding young talents, but they leave so much undiscovered and unexplored. For many students, the orthodox continuation of the traditional System, which ignores their spiritual potential and the burgeoning conceptual view of personal and creative consciousness, is beginning to fail. This continuationist tendency reminds me of the sign on the house of a Kenyan artist: **Copying Puts God to Sleep**. It certainly puts Stanislavski to sleep.

A person or idea in what philosophers refer to as a sleeping state is incapable of achieving perfection and suffers from an atrophy of inner resources. Such a state is particularly hazardous for actors. Should not the actor, as the central figure in the theatre, be permitted to evoke a new kind of creative spirit just as painters, musicians, and dancers have successfully done? Even scientists strive to sensitize their scientific instruments.

The work of Stanislavski remains the most important movement in modern acting, but it has not evolved with the same vigor and innovative turning points as other fine arts. I often have the feeling that many of the teachers influenced by Stanislavski would be more inclined to accept and appreciate a new consciousness in music or painting than they would a new consciousness in the System. Their sleep-inducing copying is in need of an awakening. They must think about the System in new ways and not fear to explore the ultimate truth of the System, even if this means departing radically from their precepts. The necessity for change is what evolution is all about. I believe that Stanislavski wanted his work to be continued for its inherent potential, having no desire to see the artistic principles which he had already discovered endlessly rehashed.

There is an inclination to associate certain changes in consciousness with the mystical realm of New Age beliefs. Though considered dubious by some, this realm is neither creatively dangerous nor the exclusive domain of spaced-out freaks. Some very fine minds in both art and science have found mystical experiences to be highly productive.

Contemporary physics provides other examples of the link between mysticism and creativity. In *The Tao of Physics*, Fritoj Capra explains that there are those physicists who lean toward a form of Eastern mysticism in order to let their minds soar into elevated states of time and space in search of flashes of insight. They seek the same kind of experience that Einstein described when, at the age of sixteen, he was struck by the image of riding through a beam of light. This mystical experience was the source of his general theory of relativity and his unimaginable creative energy.

Higher levels of consciousness are not the exclusive property of Eastern mysticism. The goal of achieving these levels is embraced by a growing number of people throughout the world. To whatever degree higher forms of consciousness are mystical, they are also universal. Stanislavski would have been both impressed and inspired by present-day experiments being conducted in Russian academies to develop "hidden human reserve capacities" and "neglected human potentials." He would surely find a way of using their discoveries to arrive at new directions for his search. He would be fascinated with recent discoveries about neuropsychological functioning, and would certainly apply this knowledge to enhance the sensitivity of the actor's nervous system.

Stanislavski's imagination suffered no inertia in refining his basic discoveries and modifying entire aspects of his System. His never-ending search for a more perfect realization of his ideas caused him to shape and reshape his theories, only to entirely abandon some of them later. Under the direction of Stanislavski's constantly leaping imagination, the System changed and evolved. His American disciples believed that their work was a continuation of Stanislavski's, as they sought to clarify those areas of the System that they believed to be most effective. I hope that the reader will regard this book as my own effort to further the contemporary potential in Stanislavski's discoveries.

The Stanislavski teachers who dote on the development of sensory perception and emotional reliving commit an injustice by not permitting actors to become aware of the creative instincts that lie beyond a mundane consciousness of the System. Major mentors of the System maintain a stranglehold on their followers, even on those who consider themselves mavericks and deny the influence of their teachers. Hard work and discipline are required to realize the boundless creative rewards of a higher level of consciousness. Stanislavski, himself, emphasized that a talent cannot achieve its artistic potential without hard work. I have found that many actors in training are both willing and capable of reaching for greater heights of consciousness—a process surely superior to the non-spiritual techniques which are put forth as the path to magical solutions—yea, unto stardom!

My only wish is that the evidence of results documented in the second part of this book will be of some benefit to actors who share my belief that they can achieve an energetic consciousness level by permitting their instruments to be a vessel for transpersonal techniques.

IS THAT ALL THE SYSTEM OFFERS?

When I began to teach in 1968, I instructed students in all the exercises I had learned and practiced. This took less than six months, though my personal study of the exercises took six years.

Although many actors had achieved great success with the same handful of exercises, I began to ask myself, "Is that all there is to help an actor create dynamic and truthful behavior?" The question gnawed at my creative curiosity. Perpetuating the tenets and assumptions of the System in the same manner in which I had learned them left me uninspired. "Surely," I ruminated, "there has to be more."

Gradually, I began to leave the shelter of what I had learned and grounded myself in a new place where my imagination could have more flesh and blood than it had previously experienced.

In the traditional teaching of the System, emotional exploration is a central goal. It is interesting to note that some leaders in New Age awareness exclude the word "emotional" from their methods of heightening consciousness. In his approach to higher levels of awareness, Jack Schwarz, an early New Age explorer, speaks of the physical, mental, and spiritual, excluding the emotional. His work was applauded by Joseph Campbell, one of the most highly regarded philosophers, teachers, and (according to some) transpersonalists of our time. Within the traditional use of the System, the main counterparts of Schwarz's theory are physical, mental and emotional. In my work, I have added the spiritual in order to reach for what Stanislavski called "the incarnation" of a role.

The spiritual quest, as shown by numerous artists, leads to a higher creative functioning. The human nervous system has the capacity to function at a much higher level. The spiritual is a necessary ingredient to tap this potential, which already exists in every actor's physical body, and channel it toward artistic growth. Reaching higher levels of consciousness in acting is not an easy matter. Just as an athlete must use physical muscle to shatter previous records, an actor must use spiritual muscle to break down barriers that prevent the attempt for the total creative awareness and growth in acting envisioned by Stanislavski as the "new life." When Stanislavski referred to the perfect actor, who "had yet to be born," some feel that he had a vision of perfection akin to Gordon Craig's idea of the super-marionette. Craig's goal is not the creation of a puppet manipulated by strings, but an actor capable of reaching full potential by mastering all the skills necessary. Through mastery of these "superskills," the actor feels a connection with the higher forces of the universe.

INNOVATIVE ARTISTS

> *If art is to nourish the roots of our culture, society must set the artist free to follow his vision wherever it takes him.*
>
> John F. Kennedy

Stanislavski had a strong belief in innovation. He believed that a person can benefit from studying the work of a predecessor and then improving on what has gone before; he objected to the tendency in some avant-garde artists to reject the past.

With artistic humility, he felt his own work provided just a few grains upon which to build. At the very beginning of the English version of his autobiography's final chapter, he refers to himself as a conservative, but acknowledges that it would be a sin not to permit young innovators the right to rebel. There are bound to be enemies in this process, he said to his comrades, whom he also regarded as conservatives.

Though "innovation" has become a newly popularized term in the jargon of late 20th century entrepreneurship, it has been a part of the evolution of any art since the beginning of time. Innovation stems from the human impulse to realize one's responsibility to improve upon what has gone before. The limits of art, like those of science, are unknown destinations, reflecting the very nature of the innovative spirit in our expanding universe. In order to keep up with that expansion, both the artist and the scientist must be iconoclasts, because conventionalities, by their very nature, find uniqueness anathematic. Looking at concepts in a new way, perceiving what no one has seen before requires a spirit as rebellious as Stanislavski's. The rebel possesses a certain necessary courage. As Joseph Campbell explained, this rebellious courage is needed to remain psychologically balanced in an insensitive world that tends to be wary of innovative processes and is often unresponsive to heroic deeds—especially those with a spiritual message.

It is generally conceded that all innovative artists have been rebels in one way or another. Rebels all break rules, but, as the composer Charles Ives believed, an artist must study the past in order to know something about the rules one wishes to break. This thought was shared by educator Robert Hutchins, head of the highly esteemed Center for the Study of Democratic Institutions. His message for the young was, "Get ready for anything, something will happen, anything may happen, and it may not be what you expect." The message is equally valid for the rebel artist who journeys into unknown realms and often brings back a vision that fosters the dynamic forces in art and in humankind. The heroic wish of the rebel is to contribute to the improvement of civilization by offering a new way to experience the world in which we create, love, and play. The evolution of any human endeavor, as Will Durant pointed out, is a process of requiring people to get out of the way in order that civilization can benefit from a vital new way of looking at its accomplishments. The artist who is brave enough to explore the unknown does not do so in deliberate defiance of what has been learned from mentors. Instead, the act of turning away from the past suggests that the artist's mentors have succeeded in showing that the world of art is one of infinite richness.

Abraham Maslow told us much about innovation; about the courage needed by innovators to defy and challenge accepted precepts; and the hostility that new concepts inevitably encounter. He underscored that innovators feel a personal responsibility for making a contribution to their world. Even though they might wish to take it easy and let someone else solve the problems they recognize, deep down they realize that if they don't take the time, no one else will.

The course of history offers innumerable examples of one generation improving upon the ideas, knowledge, and techniques of the previous generation. History represents every contribution made by individuals, and it is to history that their ideas belong. Stanislavski felt such a historical link with Riccaboni, whose book preceded *An Actor Prepares* by two hundred years.

Every individual should feel an indisputable right to make a contribution to his/her profession. Most of us want to leave our mark on the world. I feel that the artist who wishes to be original is simply seeking a way to stand in the company of the predecessors whose accomplishments were inspirational. Unfortunately, this sometimes occurs as the age-old custom of committing patricide in order to be liberated. Liberation does not demand the extinction of what has gone before, it simply requires the innovator to establish his/her own territory. Within this place, the innovator can reshape old rules to fit into a more contemporary context, while simultaneously exorcising whatever demons prevent the expression of individuality.

Often, an interval of several years lapses before there is acceptance of the innovator's rethinking, reshaping, and reinterpretation. Any theory has to be knocked around for a while. Even Hawking's theory of Black Hole Explosions was once—and by some still is—considered rubbish. New theories in art have always been assaulted and refuted before receiving acceptance. This is the experience an innovative artist must expect when taking his/her art away from the known and familiar toward the supernormal. In Vienna, Gustav Mahler suffered humiliation at the hands of the ruling circles. He pleaded with conductors to listen to his scores. After a conductor finally consented to listen to one movement of a symphony and then rejected it, Mahler could only console himself with the belief, "My time will come." As it did!

One of the great musical visionaries of our century, Arnold Schoenberg, was influenced by Mahler's musical intensity. He and the Russian painter Wassily Kandinsky were close collaborators against conventional thought in art forms. They shared a deep interest in synesthesia—a condition in which different modalities occur with the senses—colors speak and sounds are seen. Schoenberg radically broke away from centuries of traditional notions of tonality. He ended up living in Los Angeles on a $27.50 a month university pension. This same university, which once refused to give him a ground-floor office despite his doctor's advice, later became one of two universities to dedicate a building in his honor. His opera, *Moses and Aaron*, which is regarded as his masterpiece, lacks a third act because he failed to get the Guggenheim Fellowship of $2,500 that he needed to support his family. Throughout his lifetime, the ruling circles in music remained unaware of the visionary in their midst. He died with unspeakable lack of recognition. Today, of course, his archives are worth millions and the list of converts to his musical system includes Copland, Berio, Bernstein, Boulez, Dallapicolla, Sessions, Ginastera, Stockhausen, and even Stravinsky who once dismissed Schoenberg's musical system out of hand.

These are just two examples from the multitude of artistic visionaries who have encountered enormous obstacles when attempting to capture a new age spirit with a paradigmatic shift.

LOOKING AT THE SYSTEM THROUGH A NEW PRISM

I have always been compelled to look at the Stanislavski System through a new prism in order to view it in a fresh way. As a teacher attempting to find my own style, I have felt it to be my personal prerogative to filter Stanislavski's goals and ideas for the completion of his System through my own vision. I have never felt that I was "going off the deep end," as my major mentor claimed, because I was able to verify, with tremendous gratification, that my work was enabling actors to create behavioral experiences that far surpassed those offered by Stanislavski traditionalists. I do not attempt to instill students with a reverential attitude toward the System's basics, but rather have always attempted to arouse their imagination towards ever-expanding realities.

When I began to teach, I acquired a growing sense that the contemporary usage of Stanislavski's System had become inadequate, lethargic and lacked a sense of adventure. I began to suggest that we still had more to learn and benefit from Stanislavski and needed to breathe new life into his System. I went into uncharted territory in order to discover the delicate adjustments required to extract a talent from an impoverished reliance on technique. These adjustments enabled the actor to find a new aesthetic in the System, creating quantum leaps in his/her expression of talent that were unforeseen. The new System aesthetics I witnessed convinced me that I had truly not "gone off the deep end." I was never able to find out if my major mentor revised his opinion during the remainder of his life, but regardless of his personal shortcomings, I remain indebted to the kind attention he gave me in accepting me into the family fold. I retain cherishable memories, personal and and professional, too numerous to mention here. I decline to vilify his name and memory because of the alienation between us which occurred when I left his warmly protective and deeply caring side in New York by moving to Los Angeles to seek possibilities of a more remunerative livelihood than New York had ever offered me. Perhaps he felt that I abandoned him during the sad time that followed his wife's death. Shortly before her death, the three of us had privately discussed my doing research assistance for a book centering on his unsurpassable private theatre library.

In retrospect, it was my moving to California that eventually led to my special field of study and development of the transpersonal in acting. In California, I was able to experience infinitely rewarding communion with nature which is, as Stanislavski said, this planet's most gifted artist. During my first five years in California, I unceasingly explored its canyons, deserts, seashores and mountains and this exploration occurred simultaneously with the development of the creative beliefs expressed in this book. Both Stanislavski and Kandinsky were in agreement that one must return to nature for spiritual stimulation. I was not aware, in the beginning, that it would be the living force of nature which would eventually inspire the spiritual in my work.

When I presented the first edition of this book to major publishers in the early 1970's, nearly all had praise for it. "An important contribution to acting..." "We much appreciate the intellectual vitality in the manuscript..." "You should be proud of the contribution you've made..." "Stimulating and provocative..." "Potentially better than any acting book now on the market..." Yet, they declined to ask for publication rights. So, in the tradition of Thoreau, Joyce, Whitman and many others, I became my own publisher. Similarly, Koussevitzky, the Russian-American composer and champion of contemporary music, formed his own music publishing house so that he could promote what he believed to be a new force in music. The success of my students in creating new System aesthetics convinced me that I had gone to the outer limits in the potential use of the System, and I felt that a book was required to promote the new force in the System with which I had been experimenting. The enduring interest in this book and its use in England, Germany, Australia, Canada, Argentina, China, and Holland, among other countries, has given me the inspiration and the gift of time to continue to confirm and refine my viewpoint.

In 1973, only a limited number of books on acting had been published in America since the release of Stanislavski's books. Since then, the number of acting books has multiplied a hundredfold, with each one offering a personal point of view. When the 1973 edition of this book appeared in Los Angeles bookstores, it was an immediate sellout. This was considered phenomenal for an unadvertised book in a mimeographed format with an apparent lack of editing. The reviews which gradually began to appear were highly favorable, and the feedback from readers could not have been more encouraging. When I gave copies of the book to my mentors, one returned the book, one refused to accept it, and from the third, there was dead silence. They reacted as if I had assaulted their beliefs, but this was not my intention. I had merely attempted to accomplish what they said had not been done—to make the System systematic.

Stanislavski had not done so only because his concern was with the quest for solutions to remaining problems. However, he always believed that there was a need to systematize the thoughts of his predecessors and bemoaned the lack of an acting manual for theatre students. Unfortunately, his tendency to constantly change his ideas resulted in a disconnectedness within his theories. In this book, and its companion volume, *All About Method Acting*, I have attempted to give the System a consistency that it has lacked.

SYSTEMATIZING THE SYSTEM

A major Stanislavski disciple in America felt that the System was always taught in an uneven and disjointed manner.

The true artist should be able, consciously or unconsciously, to develop his/her art in a systematized manner. Systematic impulses remind oneself of imperfections and of boundaries to be crossed in order to evolve towards perfection. As Karen Horney pointed out, we have great potential for growth and are discontent if we do not actively pursue this potential. She opposed Freud's pessimistic view of humans as "destructive by nature" and possessing only the "choice to destroy or suffer." This is a belief she shared with Abraham Maslow who said, "From Freud we learned that the past exists now in the person. Now we must learn, from growth theory and self-actualization theory that the future also exists in the person in the form of ideals, hopes, duties, tasks, plans, goals, unrealized potentials, missions, fate, destiny, etc. One for whom no future exists is reduced to the concrete, to hopelessness, to emptiness."

To the onlooker, the artistic development of an artist may look helter-skelter, but for the artist there exists an orderly plan which may be too complex for the outsider to perceive. Sometimes, even the artist may be unaware of the orderly development taking place while building a career.

Hegel believed that, for each art form, there exists a corresponding science that is more important than the art itself. The science of acting involves systematic training, which requires the same discipline and dedication as any science. Some who have chosen acting as a career possess this professional attitude to an extraordinary degree, while others have it on extremely low levels.

My attempt to give the System a consistency unavoidably took me into unexplored areas where I could consider new options and alternatives. This same urge to make a contribution to the training process of the actor has continually pushed me to systematically consider newer and newer dimensions of the System. Systematic explorations require progressing from one point to another with the knowledge that any dedicated pursuit will keep evolving. I hope that the inclusion of several new exercises in this revision of *The Transpersonal Actor*, as well as the refinement of previous exercises, will convey that I have continued to evolve.

THE TRANSPERSONAL IN ACTING

Carl Jung defined "transpersonal" as a process by which one attains a higher level of consciousness. For the actor, the message is quite clear: use all of your resources to journey beyond and test the outer limits of conventional horizons. By doing so, you are keeping astride with the secret and mysterious forces that are evolving all around you.

Transpersonal philosophy is not a 20th Century invention. The philosophy has been present throughout the history of humankind. It endows us with our humanistic nature, as well as with our ability to become co-creators of the planet and with our potential to reach beyond our conscious selves.

We have been warned of the need to create a new kind of human being if our planet is to survive. We can no longer indulge our neuroses; we now have an obligation to move toward the path of higher spiritual evolution and higher states of consciousness. The level of consciousness on which most of the world finds itself today has brought us to the edge of extinction. Many feel that they are awake and aware, but closer investigation will prove otherwise. There will be resistance to rigorous self-examination. For some, an honest investigation of their beliefs would prove too much of a shock. And the world has always been full of people who are intolerant of what they do not understand.

It is difficult to estimate the number of people who have become aware of new ways of personal expansion or who are in the process of developing this awareness. Evolved Americans are leading the exploration in mind and spirit expansion which may prove to be a silent weapon in global politics. World leaders are not sufficiently aware of the potential power of this weapon. The continuing popularity of spiritual growth books reflects a burgeoning awareness that people are capable of achieving results beyond the limits of what they expect or have been willing to accept.

The transpersonal approach seeks to create a new type of functioning in the actor based on higher levels of consciousness. Some people see a relationship between transpersonal techniques and the Zen experience, which makes harsh demands upon the individual in order to realize untapped potentialities. The Zen discipline leads to a personal enlightenment. The transpersonal actor can be regarded as a Zen artist inasmuch as he/she has no desire to go through a training period, or an entire career, without realizing the heights that might be developed in the art of acting. The techniques of transpersonal acting require an inventive discipline; they are not for the inert. Their goal is a Zen-like state in which the body has become a creative "tool." In the acting section of leading theatre bookstores, one is likely to find titles such as Herrigel's *The Method of Zen* and *Zen in the Art of Archery*. Although my book shares some of the philosophical underpinnings of Herrigel's books, unlike his works, it offers practical assistance for the actor who wishes to be liberated from conventional acting techniques and to celebrate his/her creativity in a joyous new way.

My introduction of transpersonal techniques into Stanislavski precepts represents the results of my continuing search for the attainment of a more expressive and nuanced form of acting. Using these techniques, the actor reaches into inner resources and discovers that the acting instrument can be honed and harnessed to function on new artistic levels of creative consciousness. The actor becomes aware of the ultimate goal of the Stanislavski System and the true value of Stanislavski's bequest to the art of acting.

A POSTSCRIPT

I was able to test the outer limits of Stanislavski because of the abiding devotion and dedication of eighteen intelligent and talented actors who were similarly compelled to go beyond the narrow creative experiences of sensory exercises. In the upheaval years of the late 1960's, we felt in tune with the state of mind and spirit of the time as we did our own thing. After working together for five years, we presented our style in a theatre production. It was enthusiastically received by its audiences and garnered extraordinary praise from most members of the press. We had done what my mentors said was necessary; we proved the validity of transpersonal vision and theory in a theatre production. We preceded Melrose Avenue's new look by many years, and our theatre, The Zephyr, remains a Melrose showplace. I have always regarded our experience as a reward for my years of study and research. It was the type of unification of theory and practice that must occur at least once in the lifetime of a creative researcher attempting to develop a theoretical system into a practical method. When I completed the first edition of this book in 1973, I presented my eighteen "co-explorers" with a list of twelve possible titles. Unanimously, they selected *The Transpersonal Actor*.

PART II

THE TRANSPERSONAL ACTOR

Part II

Technique Exercises

CHANNELING IMPULSE EXERCISE

The sensory exercises in *All About Method Acting*, the companion volume to this book, have prepared you for adventures into unexplored areas of your acting instrument. Until now, your technique exercise work has been concerned with the senses which dominate much of your existence. The early transpersonal exercises will begin to enhance your ability to create totally new behavioral nuances beyond those offered by traditional sensory exercises.

The Channeling Impulse Exercise will permit you to sense the flow of new inner energy patterns, transforming the use of your inner sensitivities. This transformation can result in an increased creative control of the flow of inner energies and create a new artistic image. It requires that you be creatively open, as you must temporarily abandon the behavioral results you have achieved through the exclusive use of sensory technique exercises. Some do not wish to take the risk involved in changing their creative style, fearing to step into an unknown without knowing if there will be creative and professional rewards. Picasso was not afraid when he gave up cubism to travel into a succession of creative changes, even though his reputation as an artist had already been established. Like other modern artists, he had started with simple subjects—painting a still-life of an apple, a bottle or other everyday objects. Gradually, he reached his cubism stage and began to transform simple, everyday realities into richly complex forms. This initial transpersonal exercise takes you to a point of departure from familiar realities to richer behavioral values.

The sensory exercises of taste, smell and pain contact personal experiences you have had with the inner senses in order to give authenticity to your emotional behavior. The meanings you derived from those exercises are important to the Channeling Impulse Exercise. Often a localized sensorial sensation is the beginning point for this exercise. From there, its energy is transmitted to other inner areas. The sensory exercises created behavior that related to your own inner impulses; this exercise creates unfamiliar impulses that are, nevertheless, part of your organic instrument.

With this exercise, you will begin to strengthen a desire to respond to an increasing range of unfamiliar experiences. You have dwelled in your body for sometime and may be familiar with its sensory experiences, but suddenly you will discover that your inner organs, connecting tissues, autonomic nervous system and myriad cells can be charged with new energies.

Ordinarily, we feel only aches and pains that have to do with certain disturbances that take place within the body.

Aside from the pleasures of the stomach, we take too much for granted as to how the organs are feeling the rest of the time. With the Channeling Impulse Exercise you will be able to give the inner organs new experiences. The organs are part of your inner self and can be imaginatively explored for new and unfamiliar choices. You might even achieve a new understanding of the function of your inner organs and the purpose of their existence in terms of your inner life.

This exercise finds meaning in increasingly accepted forms of personal growth experiences as well as alternative medicine:

Acupuncture

Acupuncture and acupressure use the body's own energy to produce a healing flow through the 72,000 channels in the body. Although Western science has not been able to totally explain how acupuncture works, it has become more accepting of this valuable medical treatment.

Yoga

The Channeling Impulse Exercise is related to the yogic principle of transferring energies. In yoga, the pituitary gland (located at the base of the brain) can be stimulated to secrete beneficial hormones into the entire body. Stanislavski studied yoga and attempted to use its principles in the development of his System. Many never shared his interest in yoga, although his widely-used circles of attention exercise was inspired by yogic principles.

Biofeedback

This innovative discipline can improve poor circulation simply by creating warmth in one area of the body and permitting the warmth to be channeled to the cold areas afflicted with poor circulation.

Psychic Energy

The energy of top young actors has both physical and psychic qualities. Perhaps the glow of their physical persona has something to do with their psychic energy. Practitioners of psychic energy create strong, healthy auras surrounding an inner organ, such as the heart, and then permit its healthy glow to be channeled into the rest of the body.

Perhaps you have begun to regard this exercise as a tool which is not only creative but also holistically beneficial for the tip-top state of health that an actor must possess. This exercise offers a double blessing, since through its use you can create an acting choice and simultaneously improve your well-being.

The electricity of an actor's impulses plays a vital part in communicating with an audience or camera. In addition, psychological and physical attitude can change in richness and intensity as the impulse is channeled from one area to another. These electrical impulses are present in the body's multitudinous cells. As an actor you should want to know how to become acquainted with the nature of these impulses. This exercise endows you with a technique to go with an impulse rather than short-circuiting its connection with another impulse.

Therapeutic insights and benefits can be derived from the exercise. By pointing out how you may be blocking certain impulses, the exercise grants you the means to un-block them and complete their expressive nature. You also have the opportunity to examine the nature and conse-quences of blocked impulses. You can even discover how certain blocked emotions, such as aggression, can be good for your well-being as you let it travel through your body. Strongly blocked emotions definitely restrict the creative use of your instrument. In my workshop, I have encoun-tered actors conditioned to avoid the expression of aggres-sive emotions. The goal for such people is not to regard the emotion in a negative way but to find out about its positive aspects.

The exercise can also reveal how everyday impulses create facial and body mannerisms. A mannerism can be the result of hiding certain impulses and therefore can be a rich source of locked-up expression. This exercise seeks to change mannerisms into bolder and clearer expressions. You can benefit greatly during initial experiments with this exercise by pinpointing possible areas of locked-up expres-sions. Create sensations in those areas and release them during the course of the exercise.

Be prepared for a sudden change in the quality of your acting experience. Even actors who have not fully responded to sensory exercises find with the Channeling Impulse Ex-ercise that floodgates suddenly open as the richness of their sensitivities begins to be used in a more imaginative and creative way. This exercise, therefore, offers invaluable means to deal with problems of feelings that were not refined during the sensory work.

Finally, the best acting occurs when a true relationship between impulse and expression replaces uncontrolled emotion. This exercise intends to give you the artistic skill to create that desirable relationship.

THE CHANNELING IMPULSE EXERCISE

You may wish to refer to the examples and choices which begin on page 67 in order to have a fuller image of the essence of a Channeling Impulse.

1. Select an action. An action list appears in the appendix.
2. Select an emotion for the action.

Love	Envy
Tenderness	Impatience
Sexual Excitement	Obstinacy
Sympathy	Guilt
Pity	Despair
Anxiety	Anger
Shame	Helplessness
Sadness	Joy
Confidence	Hope
Pride	Passion
Hopelessness	Hate
Greed	Serenity
Fear	Depression
Rage	Numbness
Courage	Compassion

3. Select a sensation, sensory or otherwise, which you feel is related to the emotion.

   Examples:

   To get all I can
   Emotion: Anxiety
   Original area: Itchy feet
   Predetermined area: Face

   To plow through the blizzard
   Emotion: Impatience
   Original area: Power line buzz in right hand
   Predetermined area: Left calf

   To provoke
   Emotion: Tenderness
   Original area: Taste in mouth
   Predetermined area: Chest

   To listen
   Emotion: Sadness
   Original area: Sensation in left knee
   Predetermined area: Chin

   To hold my ground
   Emotion: Pride
   Original area: Hot oil in crotch
   Predetermined area: Cheek bones

Guidelines for the Channeling Impulse Exercise

...Permit the choice to reside in a localized area somewhere in the body. This is referred to as the original area where you internally experience the nature of the choice. Don't be afraid of using unfamiliar sensations in the original area. You can even select and reproduce an experience which has occurred in another part of your body as some of the examples will illustrate.

...There is a purpose served when you maintain a sensation in the original area. The need to maintain it is not dissimilar to that of the giant iguanas of the Galapagos Islands who can bring their blood to their center to conserve body heat.

...It is preferable and more effective to create sensations originating inside the body. However, if you choose an external choice, such as sun on the head, then it is important that the sensation move inside the head.

...Maintain the sensation in the original area while relaxing the rest of the body, particularly the predetermined area to which you will first channel the impulse. Be mindful of any anticipated sensation in the predetermined area.

...Do not rush the exercise by releasing it without sufficient exploration in either the original area or the predetermined area.

...Release the sensation from the original area and allow it to travel through areas of relaxation into the predetermined area. Avoid being mental about its passage. If the sensation has been strong in the original area, it should be strong when arriving at the predetermined area. If not, you may be retaining some of the sensation in the original area.

...When you have channeled the sensation into the pre-determined area, relax the original area and other areas through which the sensation has traveled on its way to the predetermined area. The sensation now replicates itself in the predetermined area. Sense the change that is caused in the predetermined area. Permit it to remain there as long as you wish.

...Release the sensation from the predetermined area and let it travel into the body, journeying to wherever it wishes. For a specific behavioral purpose, you can release the sensation from the predetermined area on a particular word or line of dialogue. Eleanora Duse has been described as having the ability to begin a sensation in her toes and then move it upwards into her head area before releasing it into her famous smile.

...For subtle behavioral purposes, create the sensation in an area and release small amounts of it into another area. For example, gradually let a sensation in the stomach rise to the face. A certain expression on the face can be gradually increased in strength as more sensation from the stomach rises to the face area. This can be particularly useful for a film closeup given the ability of a camera to capture subtle changes in facial expression.

...When the sensation has been released from the prede-termined area, play with it over long distances as it travels from one hidden area of the body to another. Determine the way in which your selected emotion is affected as the impulse moves around. Is it intensified or weakened? If it weakens, it may become intensified again upon moving into another area. These different experiences create nuanced behavior.

...Re-examine the predetermined area and discover whether all of the sensation has been released.

...As the energy of the impulse courses its way through your system, be intrigued by the physical and psychological effects. Sense the electrical communication of the nerve cells in the nervous system as an impulse shoots from one area to another. Trap it in areas and later release it to another area of entrapment.

...Permit the impulse to pass through communication centers as you shift it from one center to another. There are various centers that can be passed through as the impulse travels from the right elbow to the left foot, the back of the neck to the knees, or the toes to the shoulder.

...Let the impulse energize the extremities. The impulse can affect the fingers and create spontaneous gestural detail.

...Create the rhythms desired as you transmit the sensation of your choice. Be aware of your ability to steer the impulses so that they do not get out of control. Sometimes a talent can get confused by the rich response to certain impulses. This exercise offers a way of dealing with that concern.

...When you experience a sensation or stimulus in life, such as a lump in the throat or butterflies in the stomach, immediately channel that sensation elsewhere. You may discover that the sensation can have the same intensity in two different areas or that the sensation might even be stronger in another inner area.

...In later stages of experimenting with this exercise, omit the predetermined area and permit the sensation of the original area to suddenly project itself into the entire body.

There are numerous ways to experiment with the Channeling Impulse Exercise and as you express your own individuality, you will, naturally, arrive at your own ideas.

Examples

Emotion	Choice in Original Area	Predetermined Area
Love	Pelvis	Eyes
Laughter	Itch on top of head	Throat
Compassion	Brilliant warmth in stomach	Head
Fear	Solar plexus	Shoulders
Flippancy	Genitals	Top of head
Confidence	Sunshine in head	Chest
Envy	Cold hands	Eyes
Pride	Taste in mouth	Back of neck
Anxiety	Severe pain in groin	Head
Hopelessness	Taste in mouth	Stomach
Shame	Smell	Chest
Impatience	Itch in left toe	Both hands
Sympathy	Objects in hands	Back of neck
Tenderness	Taste in mouth	Chest
Guilt	Taste in mouth	Right hand
Greed	Itchy hands	Both feet
Depression	Upset stomach	Head
Courage	Electric current in arms	Entire body

Emotion	Choice in Original Area	Predetermined Area
Sexual	Anatomical object in pelvis	Hands
Rage	Fire in chest	Head
Despair	Bitter taste in mouth	Stomach
Joy	Sound in solar plexus	Cheeks
Pride	Hot tension in tailbone	Eyes
Guilt	Flutter in heart	Thighs
Confidence	Warm beam of light in base of brain	Base of Spine
Serenity	Sunshine inside head	Extremities
Greed	Cold chill in spine	Eyes
Envy	Electricity in sinuses	Feet
Numbness	Cheeks	Abdomen

Choices for Body Areas

HEAD

Headache to stomach
Sensation in head to body
Tension in head to shoulders
Itch on top of head to throat
Warmth in head to heart

Explosion in head to hands
Headache to mouth
Sound in head to pelvis
Sound to stomach
Pounding in brain to stomach

OTHER HEAD AREAS

Aching in jaw to temples
Numbness in lips to chest
Tension in temples to stomach
Pain in eyes to back
Taste in mouth to back of neck
Tightness between temples to legs
Burning in eyes to stomach
Pain in jaw to forehead
Stiffness in jaw to stomach
Sunshine in head to both legs
Pain in cheekbones to eyes
Throbbing in temples to legs
Sound to third eye

NECK AND THROAT

Warmth in back of neck to throat
Warmth in neck to shoulder
Neckache to small of back
Dry throat to stomach
Taste in throat to lips
Parched throat to stomach
Pain in neck to face

Energy in neck to eyes
Tightness in throat to feet
Thirst in throat to ears

SHOULDERS

Warmth in shoulder blades to forehead
Cold in shoulders to hands
Energy in shoulders to arms and hands
Pain in right shoulder to head
Stiffness in shoulders to face

CHEST

Warm chest to back of neck
Sexual feeling in chest area to eyes
Numbness in breast to face
Tightness in chest to cheekbones
Heat in chest to face and ears

HEART

Energy from heart to third eye
Erratic heartbeat to head
Palpitations to head
Strong, steady heartbeat to head
Heartache to mouth and hands
Erratic heart to legs
Racing heart to head
Heartache to hands
Rapid heartbeat to upper spine

STOMACH AREA

Nausea in stomach to feet
Upset stomach to face
Laughter from diaphragm to face
Full stomach to base of brain
Butterflies in stomach to face
Hunger pangs to pelvic area
Nervous stomach to eyes
Electricity from stomach to eyes
Stomachache to eyeballs
Electric energy from stomach to throat
Queasiness in stomach to fingertips
Full stomach to armpits
Brilliant warmth in stomach to fingertips
Queasiness in stomach to temples
Fullness in stomach to face
Stomachache to head
Cramps in stomach to legs
Queasiness in stomach to knees
Sensation in lower intestine to chest cavity

BACK AND SIDES

Cold chill up spine and through eyes
Stiffness in spine to neck
Pain in back to face
Energy from lower spine to face
Ache in left side to both shoulders
Warmth from base of spine up through spinal column
  and into head

PELVIS AND GROIN

Sensation in pelvis to left hand
Sensation in pelvis to eyes
Pain in groin to head
Sensation in groin to eyes
Hot wine in the veins to heart

SEXUAL AREA

Sexual arousal to chest and shoulders
Sexual excitement to mouth
Warm genitals to face
Sexual arousal into the veins
Sexual warmth to chest
Horny hot flashes to eyes

LIMBS AND HANDS

Nervous fingers to bridge of nose
Pain in hand to face
Itchy hands to nose
Warmth in hands to shoulders
Clammy hands to back of neck
Sensation in upper limbs to eyes
Heat in fingers to chest

LEGS AND FEET

Impatience in legs to cheekbones
Tickling feet to nose

Itchy feet up the legs
Stiffness in knees to shoulders
Warmth in feet to head
Itchy feet to mouth
Itchy feet to hands
Pain in feet to stomach
Cold feet to chest
Numbness in feet to arms

THE DOUBLE CHANNELING IMPULSE EXERCISE

Select two choices which have different and opposite emotions. Try not to think of them as conflicting. Instead, permit them to merge and create unexpected emotions.

Examples

Anger—Serenity
Compassion—Reserve
Release—Suppress
Courage—Fear

There are two ways in which you can work with the opposite choices:

1. Create them in the original areas and simultaneously release them into the predetermined areas.

2. Create the sensation of one of the emotions and release it to the predetermined area. While it re-

mains in the predetermined area, create the sensation of the opposite choice in its original area.

Release the first choice from the predetermined area and the second choice from its original area to the predetermined area.

3. There are different ways to do this somewhat complex, but richly rewarding exercise, and you can arrive at your own ideas.

Examples

Hope: White light in ears to knees
Despair: Burning sensation in abdomen to mouth

Euphoria: Sexual excitement in clitoris to throat
Hunger: Base of spine to legs

Guilt: Flutter in heart to thighs
Pride: Headache to hands

Concern: Warm oil in head to hands
Flippancy: Low energy charge in chest to legs

Love: Warm sensation of genitals to back of head
Stiffness: Cold water in navel to toe tips

Gentleness: Perfume in sinus to throat and chest
Realization: Debussy music in ears to hands and fingers

Serenity: Energy from heart to third eye
Flippancy: Sourness in pelvis to mouth

Rage: Fire from chest to head
Frustration: Numbness in right hand to left foot

Compassion: Brilliant warmth in stomach to head
Frustration: Cold knees to feet

Courage: Electric current in arms into body
Fear: Icy water in stomach veins and into body

Sincere: Cold chill running up spine and through eyes
Flippancy: Pelvis to mouth

Laughter: Stomach to throat
Tears: Throat to eyes

Sex: Crotch to top of head
Hesitancy: Shoulder to shoulder

Laughing: Top of head to throat
Crying: Stomach to eyes

Hunger: Diaphragm to chest
Complacency: Groin to eyes

Pleasure: Groin to face
Pain: Ache in shoulder to stomach

Joy: Tingling in feet to throat
Pain: Left elbow to right elbow

Love: Pelvis to eyes
Hate: Headache to mouth

Euphoria: Light in head to stomach
Heavy Tension: Thigh to shoulders

Pleasure: Groin to face
Pain: Shoulders to arms

Anger: Chest to face
Serenity: Sun in head to body

Fear: Solar plexus to shoulder blades
Courage: Crotch to eyes

Sincerity: Ear to ear via back of neck
Flippancy: Genitals to top of head

Compassion: Energy from heart to third eye
Reserve: Ice water in spine

Calm: Warm chest to back of neck
Nervous: Nervous fingers to bridge of nose

Compassion: Brilliant warmth from stomach to head
Frustration: Cold knees to feet

Courage: Electric current in arms into entire body
Fear: Solar plexus to shoulder blades

SPATIAL OBJECTS EXERCISE

Exercises of sensorial stimulation in the Stanislavski System relate to how we are affected by various stimuli in the environment: odors, sounds, sights, objects and varying degrees of temperature. The Spatial Objects Exercise creates environmental forces which are not necessarily registered in sensorial experience. However, your imagination can create them and make them exist as strongly as any sensory experience. As Joseph Campbell said, "We think about space."

Your creative consciousness is capable of experiencing new and imaginary realities. Your actual sensory realities are limited to your real-life experiences. Imaginary realities that you create permit you to experience sensations which you were not consciously aware you could have. This exercise also greatly multiplies the tactile stimuli available for physical behavior and sensations. For that reason, latent visceral qualities will open up with new physical nuances and more imaginative texture. Your willingness to experience your choices will aid in creating behavior that is fresh, spontaneous and unpredictable.

The nature of your choices for this exercise should be tactile; there is no need to dwell on other sensorial aspects of the objects. The aim of the exercise is to enable you to extend your range of tactile experiences. This requires creating imaginary phenomena that can have powerful realities. A new mode of consciousness develops as you become more acquainted with the existence of new streams of energy enveloping you.

Once I had gone beyond the boundaries of traditional technique exercises, this exercise was a natural step in the sequence of new exercises. Sensorial acting choices have both inner and outer values. The Channeling Impulse Exercise is designed to create new inner values. It is followed by the Spatial Objects Exercise which has the power to create new outer values.

The words of painter Georges Braque assisted me as this exercise coalesced. He said, "All my life my great concern has been to paint space." Not only did he succeed in painting space, but he was also able to make the viewer feel a sensuous substance. Similarly, Antonin Artaud supported the nature of this exercise by implying that an actor's physical language should make space speak.

The use of this exercise can be illuminating as an experimental choice for a character you are creating. Part of role building is to know how the character relates to space and its boundaries. This exercise is not unlike working with the expanding or narrowing circles of attention that Stanislavski describes in *An Actor Prepares*.

In the early development of this exercise, I reflected that space had not been adopted into the System as a valid means of creating behavior. In sensorial techniques used to create tactile physicalities, an actor selects choices from familiar environmental experiences. In the Spatial Objects Exercise, you can use a fantasy approach to space and create a variety of imaginary forces. The imaginary forces you contact can shape your acting instrument and produce an unusual behavioral presence.

Renowned physicists have viewed the macroscopic space that surrounds us and have explained how space vibrates with activities which are part of our existence. Some physicists have been particularly drawn to the Zen concept of space being a breathing and living continuum.

For example, the aesthetics of Zen painting is to enter into a painting and sense its motion.

In this exercise you acquaint yourself with the dynamic and unseen forces that perpetually besiege the human condition. Our multitude of nerve endings are constantly having tactile contact with these unseen energy streams. They are powerful because, to a great extent, we depend upon them to trigger our energy sources. Some elements in our environment are composed of cosmic energies which give us sustenance. We draw them into our body for the same reason that we drink water or eat food. The Spatial Objects Exercise will demonstrate how aspects of your human conditioning make you aware or unaware of invisible forces acting upon you.

Following thorough sensory training, you are ready to venture into the territory of this exercise in which you can experience sudden physical explosions of new tactile sensations.

The choices for the exercise should affect the entire body. Your primary concern is to acquire knowledge for creating a new language in the acting space you inhabit. The exercise also has a way of specifically pointing out your vulnerabilities and defenses. You deal with those as you dissolve the boundaries which keep the energy of your choices from making tactile contact with your body. You may even experience the phenomenon of spatial clairvoyance.

THE SPATIAL OBJECTS EXERCISE

1. Select an action which conveys the motivation and meaning you wish to examine.
2. Select a choice from the following suggestions or create your own after reviewing the list.

Action	*Spatial Objects*
To admire	Different color balloons
To remain on my feet	Flying arrows
To figure out	Abstract paintings
To resist	Attacking people
To reject	Infectious people
To hesitate	Spears
To smash	Spider webs
To find protection	Blankets
To cast off the yoke	Bugs
To see beyond	Mirrors
To put something over	Masks
To take a chance	Nazi SS officers with machine guns
To scorn	Syringes
To fight poachers	Wounded animals
To win them over	Scooping seagulls
To cool things off	Sticks of burning incense
To resist	Darts
To brush off	Corn silk
To be self-concerned	Barbed wire
To make light of inner pain	Pounding fists
To keep things my way	Falcons

Action

To win my place
To obscure
To squirm through
To persevere
To discover the truth
To surmount
To have the power

Spatial Objects

Jabbing fingers
Hypnotizing hands
Unknown faces
Gremlins with sticking pins
Waves of knowledge
Rocks of different sizes
Particles of comet tails

Choice Selections

Animals
Insects
Knives
Various hands
Tumbleweed
Pellets of steam
Slimy walls
Giant hammers
Snowballs
Electrical sparks
Sticky rubber objects
Laughing mouths
Spotlights
Slow-moving bubbles
Floating balloons
Giant dollar bills
Sexual organs
A person duplicated
Little green men
Caressing hands

Good spirits
Meteors
Needles
Lasso ropes
Religious spirits
Birds
Pieces of flesh
Swirls of chiffon
Colony of lepers
Bees
Ice cubes
Fighter planes
Plants
Fantasy objects
Animal eyes
Holographs
Frisbees
Clouds
Cosmic rays
Feathers

Hands of children	Globs of jello
Man-eating ants	Butterfly wings
Red and green flashing lights	Snakes
Feather dusters	Stubby fingers
Light beams	Hovering knives
Mouths	Silver cords
Cotton puffs	Sacred tablets
Down pillows	Wood carvings
People applauding and booing	Aurora Borealis

Guidelines for the Spatial Objects Exercise

...Unlike the Personal Object and Wandering Personal Object Exercises described in *All About Method Acting*, you do not make direct contact with your choice with your hands or other parts of your body. You grant your choice the freedom to make contact with you. A helpful image from nature is the way wind sculpts sand dunes with varying shapes and forms. Let your choices have the varying rhythmic powers of wind as you permit the objects to be a shaping force and give your instrument fluid forms. Imagine the objects as tools belonging to a sculptor and your body as the material with which the tools create living shapes. As you may have concluded, this exercise attempts to depart from the prosaic results often attained by overall sensorial sensations of heat, cold, etc.

...Permit Spatial Objects to engulf you as they approach you from above, below, back, front and sides; permit them to contact you at different angles. Let the space around you breathe with the energies of your choices as they contact you with varying degrees of force or tenderness. Let the choices agitate your acting instrument; experience the texture of the physical impulses they create. The important factor is to get involved with the objects as they affect every part of your body. By submitting your body completely to the objects, you will gain a new ability to create within your imagination tactile behavior unlike any you may have previously experienced.

...Permit yourself to be surrounded by objects that are trying to envelop you in ways that can be loving, destructive or mystifying. Let the objects break through any barriers you have consciously or unconsciously created between your body and the objects. Even if you do not particularly enjoy the nature of certain objects, go with your imagination and discover how the spatial abrasion inherent in objectionable objects can give you a stronger presence.

...Avoid contacting the objects visually. Let the objects contact you without attempting to see them. Be like a child with your choices. A child creates toys out of a variety of objects by permitting them to be playful.

...Permit the objects to have different rhythms and motions. Can they assail you so strongly that standing becomes difficult? Can they make you melt away? Do you have faith in the power of the objects that contact and surround you? You have created them within your fantasy and now must believe in their presence and realities.

...After you have completed a few exercises, you no longer need to submit your body completely to the objects. There can now be synergic exploration between the objects and your muscles, limbs, etc. Develop a sense of your body parts having a lively interaction with the objects. If certain choices cause parts of your body to contract, you can rid yourself of any tightness by using the muscles of the contracted area (such as the stomach, torso or pelvis) to contact the object.

...Negative choices can affect you, but don't shrink away or physically tense up. If you do, the behavioral results you seek will be diminished. For a richly complex and sensitive action, permit choices in the space around you to affect you in varying ways: loving, hateful, aggressive, sexual, fearful, etc.

...You can also duplicate a single object many times in your imagination. You may wish, for example, to duplicate a person so that there are numerous "copies" of the person. If you are duplicating parts of a person, let the parts relate to visible or hidden feelings you have about the person. You can also permit parts of a person (e.g. hands, lips, erotic parts) to proclaim feelings the person has about you. Any mixed feelings about a certain part of a person (maybe you don't like the person's nose) will lead you to multi-layered nuances. Let various parts of a person contact you in different ways—lovingly on your face, suspiciously on your back and aggressively in your pelvic area.

...The exercise can reveal fixed behavior—the involvement or lack of involvement you have in your daily life. Discover any possible fixed role you may have in your spatial orientation and how environmental objects affect you with feelings of isolation, intense sexuality, claustrophobia, etc. Determine which objects you will not permit to enter into your spatial world and the reasons for their exclusion. Then permit the objects to enter into your space, make contact with you and affect you in a way which you perhaps have never experienced.

...You can also work with sensory characteristics of the

objects. Once you have established the tactile response, focus on other ways of being stimulated by your choice. Create the sound of the objects as they approach you. Imagine how they smell. Establish their taste as they enter or try to enter your mouth. Experience sound differently as the objects plug up your ears.

Some actors don't know one part of their body from another. The bottom line of the exercise is, therefore, an enhanced richness of expression in every part of your body. Don't be an actor who doesn't know your butt from your elbow. "Acting is to perform, to be the part; to be it in your arms, your legs; to be what you are acting; to be it all over, that is acting," said the Irish-American dramatist and actor Dion Boucicault.

INTROJECTION EXERCISE

The process of introjecting people into the fabric of our personalities can formulate indelible traits. It is a process we all undergo. The actor also has this experience whenever he/she attempts to enter into the inner and outer essence of a character. The creative power of introjecting another person permits you to get totally out of yourself.

The process of introjecting people for creative and other purposes is an ancient one. Alexander the Great introjected the image he had of the legendary warrior Achilles; Leonardo da Vinci followed people around for hours and introjected expressions which he incorporated into his painting of *The Last Supper*.

Therapeutic and spiritual growth programs encourage

one to summon the spirit of someone who has qualities that are desired. This could be a religious figure or even Rembrandt, Einstein or a remarkable athlete. A devout Christian sees Christ in every person, even in a street person— perhaps especially so. By such spiritual practice, a Christian enters into a Christ consciousness in the same way that a Buddhist enters into a Buddha consciousness. The incomparable musician, Ray Charles, introjected Nat King Cole. Charles said that he breathed Cole, ate him, drank him and tasted him day and night until he was able to find his own style of musicianship.

Introjecting is often referred to as a "stealing process." George C. Scott admits that he has "stolen" from admired performances of other actors. Stravinsky admitted "stealing" from Mozart but claimed that he had the right to do so because he loved Mozart's music. The Chinese swimming team at the 1988 Summer Olympics improved their swimming skill by watching videos of Greg Louganis. Motion picture critic David Denby speculated that Peter O'Toole incorporated traits of Richard Burton, John Barrymore and Errol Flynn for his stylish performance in *My Favorite Year*.

The use of introjection in the career of outstanding performers is enlightening:

Brando said, "Actors have to observe, and I enjoy that part of it. They have to know how much spit you've got in your mouth and where the weight of your elbows is. I could sit all day in the Optimo Cigar Store telephone booth on 42nd Street and just watch the people pass by."

Guiness related, "When I was a young student...I took to following people because some instinct in me said, 'Follow! You may find out something about that person.' That is what I used to do one hour each day, like a detective...I'd begin to be in the kind of mood they were in, and beyond mood, know something of their nature."

Olivier introjected Americans to great advantage. The Milwaukee-born Alfred Lunt was his role model at the beginning of his career. While creating the role of Richard III, Olivier introjected the American director Jed Harris, whom he referred to as the most repulsive person he had ever worked with.

Robert DeNiro, in the early stages of his career, carefully studied all of Brando's films. Tom Selleck, has been described as having an acting style that incorporates features of Clark Gable and Sean Connery. The fine British actor, Jeremy Irons, said that he has emulated different actors to achieve qualities in his personal style and mentions Olivier, Guiness, Brando, Scofield and O'Toole.

The magnificent diva Maria Callas resorted to an introjecting process after a cruel critic in Verona reviewed her performance in *Aida*. He wrote that he couldn't tell her legs from the legs of the elephants on stage. She vowed to shed her obesity and took the 98-pound Audrey Hepburn as an introjection image. Her physical transformation stunned everyone.

Helen Hayes, in her most well-known stage role of Queen Victoria, patterned the role after her grandmother. On a London street, her grandmother had seen Queen Victoria passing by in her wedding procession and, over a period of time, adopted some of Queen Victoria's traits.

After 20 years in regional and summer theatres, Sada Thompson achieved overnight Broadway stardom in the play *Twigs*, in which she portrayed four different characters with startling dissimilarities on the same night. She said that during rehearsals she had to get inside the characters and often thought of people she knew, like her grand-mother and neighbors. She thought of them constantly so that they gradually got inside of her and took over.

Beginning actors often tend to capture the image of celebrated acting personalities with the hope of attaining an instant commercial image. This has caused the marketplace to be flooded with innumerable photostat copies of stars whose personally distinctive acting style has captured audience attention. This attempt by beginners can be a trap, interfering with the blooming of their own distinctive style. Therefore, beginning actors should be extremely aware of achieving a balance between their own qualities and the desired qualities of another.

Guidelines for the Introjection Exercise

...For your first attempt at this exercise, select an important person from your past, preferably your mother or father, whom you feel has traits which you have introjected. Even if you have never thought that you possess traits of your parents, the exercise may reveal that you have acquired some of their traits without being aware of it. We are, to an extent, reflections of our parents. This was revealed to an extremely intelligent actress in my workshop when, experimenting with this exercise for the first time, she introjected her mother. The actress had been through growth programs and therapy alternatives which never completely illuminated the fact, much to her chagrin, that her mother continued to have a strong hold on her. Some of the details that were present when she introjected her mother were an undeniable part of her personality, despite her dislike of them. This affirms that the exercise does reveal that we pattern ourselves after our parents, either consciously or unconsciously, and the results can be desirable or undesirable.

...During the beginning stages of this exercise you can also include childhood playmates and grade school teachers. Later, you may want to introject people that you have recently met, or even people that you do not know personally, such as TV talk show personalities whom you have observed incalculable times.

...When you introject someone important in your life, determine how you are affected by their particular psyche. Is it positive or negative? Make an effort to get the interior sense of the person. Create the particular sensory realities that the person has. By creating the inner life of a person you also will make direct contact with the driving action of their personality.

...During our work together, Cicely Tyson told me that in order to feel a character she had to get under the character's skin until it was skin tight. This points out the creative desirability of feeling the skin and nerves of an introject as your own. With this kind of exploration, the person possesses you and shapes behavioral elements.

...Actors are typically observant—and often extremely compassionate—in their relations with people from every walk of life. Every person gains significance as a model of human behavior. Each day, the TV news shows salt-of-the-earth people conveying great emotional power in response to events in their lives. Get inside the human simplicity of an unsophisticated and plain person who arouses your interest and compassion. Attempt to make direct contact with their inner experience and feelings. By doing so, you form a psychobiography about the person's inner self.

...Use your actor's keen powers of observation to create behavioral details that have to do with the stimuli and phobias that affect an introject: rapid heart beat, perspiring hands, butterflies in the stomach, weakness in the knees. (Other stimuli choices are listed in *All About Method Acting*.) Try to create the rush of adrenalin that goes through a person when a panic attack is triggered. When defining a stimulus such as butterflies in the stomach, create butterflies with a long wing span to sense the distress of such a stimulus. In dealing with an introject's phobias, try to understand how phobias can create extreme feelings of hyperventilation, bringing you almost to the edge of fainting.

THE INTROCOMBO EXERCISE

For this exercise you combine traits of several people to approximate your image of a particular character for whom a single introject will not give you all the tangibles.

Examples

To discover a new way
1.   Head and voice
2.   Arms and hands
3.   Hips

To search for what I want
1.   Facial
2.   Arms, hands and legs
3.   Torso

To quell their anxieties
1. Eyes and mouth
2. Hands and shoulders
3. Legs

In the creation of a character, sometimes you may only wish to use external features of a person and at other times, only the interior—or you can create a mixture of external and internal features. The introjection of a person's facial features can automatically summon forth other features of the person.

THE INTROCOMBO-COMBO EXERCISE

In this exercise, you depart from what may seem like simple patterning and compose bold and complex characters. You add other choices to your introject which alone may not give you the complete sense of a character. Added choices can enhance an unusual feature.

Examples

To tantalize
1. Head and hands
2. Rest of body

    IMO—Luminous cowrie shell

    Visual of an iguana

To nurture
1. Mouth and eyes
2. Arms and legs

    Smell—Pine tree

    Sound—Classical vocal music

To question
1. Head, neck and shoulders
2. Entire body except for head, neck and shoulders

    Sp. Obj.—Eyes and numbers

    Place—Visual of an arid dry plain

In my workshop, I have observed that the Introjection Exercise can be more useful than the Characterization Exercise described in *All About Method Acting*. The Characterization Exercise is extremely useful when you are not able to introject features of certain people for a character you are creating.

Introjecting others is a form of mimicry and if you have a mother who mimicked others as superbly as Robert Duvall's mother, then you can perhaps attain his engrossing sense of character details while exploring this exercise.

OUTER SPATIAL OBJECTS EXERCISE

Every emerging field creates its own language, either by developing a whole new terminology or by forging new definitions for pre-existing terms. If you have read popular books on modern physics, you have encountered such constructions as event horizon, pair creation, cosmological constant, no boundary condition and quantum thermodynamics. In the process of developing these new exercises, I have had to create an appropriate terminology. I did not ponder upon the names of these exercises for any extended period of time. In retrospect, I recall that the names emerged spontaneously, often before the exercises themselves. Some of these names may seem strange and unfamiliar to you, but I trust that you will not look askance at them. For me, the expansion of the language of acting was as necessary as the evolution of the System itself.

In conducting the research for this new edition, again and again I was reminded of things I had forgotten about Stanislavski's own experiments with his exercises. During his period of yogic studies, he evolved a prana ray emission exercise. Prana energy is often described as having powers of radiation, frequencies and electrical transmissions. Stanislavski's interest in ray emissions illustrates the spiritual growth principles inherent in his thought. In the exercise, he had actors sit in a circle and transmit energy to one another without words or sounds. Its purpose was to strengthen inner spiritual values between actors and in relation to their environment.

The Outer Spatial Objects Exercise represents a new stage of development. More than the three initial transpersonal exercises, it seeks interconnections with potential human powers—the very same kind of powers Stanislavski attempted to develop in his ray emission experiments. This exercise has the same purpose as Stanislavski's experiment: to enrichen communication between you and your environment of actors, scenery, camera and audience. Its intention is to help you discover and refine your possession of this human potential gift. It offers an intriguing exploratory process during which you gain greater insight into your own hidden energies. It advances your progress toward a more effective and expressive acting instrument. The exercise offers you a refined way of becoming aware of your unexplored creative resources and enhances your ability to intelligently gauge their power.

Your body houses electrical force which you can transmit by the use of your conscious will; this exercise grants you more conscious control of your instrumental energies. You will quickly discover rich acting subtleties as you transmit hidden energies to create rhythmic frequencies and spatial dimensions. The exercise seeks to have you experience a different kind of connectedness with the acting space you inhabit. In the System's basic exercise of creating a place, you connected with visual elements through the powers of visualization. The Outer Spatial Objects Exercise connects you with your acting space as you radiate energies from within you into the environment that encompasses you.

It is an ideal exercise for dealing with any degree of stage fright that you may have. Even Olivier struggled with bouts of stage fright. Through your conscious will, you can effect a cure for stage fright by emitting energies which touch the audience and camera rather than allowing the energies of the audience and camera to touch you. Stage fright chiefly occurs when you sense disheartening, negative energy from the force field that surrounds you.

In my workshop, I have seen actors gain an improved physical tone and presence when exploring this exercise. With remarkable consistency, the flow of energies from an actor's instrument results in increased physical prowess and effortless acting. These energy-charged emissions produce an exceptionally rich chemistry.

Prayer, chanting, ESP, remote viewing and harmonic convergence are forms of concentration related to vibrations that can be transmitted to intimate or distant points. Tibetan spiritual healers can, after a particular type of concentration, touch their patients and permit energies to enter into afflicted areas. Eastern disciplines emphasize the use of energy sources within the body, such as chakras, which enable one to make contact with higher and more human levels of consciousness and away from the animal instincts of a lower level.

Michelangelo's drawings depict various parts of the human anatomy such as the arms, hands, sometimes a thumb, muscles of the biceps, thighs, calves, etc. A study of his drawings can be helpful in noting the definition and energy in one part of the body while the rest of the body is faintly sketched.

Examples of the relationship between inner energies and physical accomplishments are plentiful in the world of outstanding athletes and artists. Recall a spectacular cross-court basket you have witnessed, and think about it in terms of the basketball player's ability to concentrate inner energies on that distant target. Similarly, a Zen archer can guide the arrow to the center of a target—even with his/her eyes closed! You can probably also think of supreme ballet dancers who let energy out through their toes when they stretch their legs. The Outer Spatial Objects Exercise attempts to simulate these uses of inner energies.

Some philosophies and disciplines focus on lifting energies from the base of the spine and permitting them to travel up the spine to the transpersonal point located at the center of the top of the head. The energy is then released into the force field existing in the sphere above the head. Some have found personal benefit in ridding the brain of unwanted thoughts by excommunicating them into the outer sphere above the head.

As a creative researcher, I have relied on behavioral results to verify the creative usefulness of an exercise. With the Outer Spatial Objects Exercise, I have witnessed outcomes which are wondrous.

One of the most extraordinary results was when an actor chose to radiate energy from his eyes. His exploration of this exercise brought me to the edge of my chair, with my mouth agape in wonderment, as I beheld him emitting white beams from his eyes. I had to tell myself that I was not hallucinating but was witnessing a phenomena. I was deeply grateful that the actor had given me the hidden truth of the exercise, just as the truth of other exercises has been revealed to me in startling ways by actors apparently already in tune with higher levels of human abilities.

Using energy from the heart and testicles; an actor created an unusual combination of sensual and sexual feelings.

Another actor, who admitted having tendencies to think more than to feel, achieved an increased physical tone by releasing energies from his hips and mouth. He created a palpable, but graceful presence as he was drawn gently in the direction of the energies emanating from his mouth and hips.

Chet Walker, who belongs to the Basketball Hall of Fame, studied with me for a year before going into film production. His gentle and sensitive nature was extremely heightened during this exercise. He used the same concentrational power he had projected into a basketball. Later, his acting began to assume the dramatic stature of Paul Robeson.

An actor attempting to develop his chest resonance was able to emit strong resonant waves from his chest area.

An international dancer discovered the telepathic properties of this exercise during an incident when she had scolded her teenage son for having removed the patina from a 400 year-old Buddha statue she had recently acquired. The son thought she would like it better if it were "cleaned up." He had hoped to surprise her with its shiny new look. She was so angry that she told him that she never wanted to see the statue again. Stricken with remorse, her son went to his room. In her own room, she began to feel regret for her behavior toward her son, not having considered his chronic state of mental depression. She began to radiate parts of herself through the large house and into his room, visualizing her energy soothing her son. When they saw each other again, a little later, her son remarked that he sensed an energy enter into his room and was extremely comforted. Through this exercise she had discovered her own hidden force to heal, as others have discovered such powers through prayer, chanting and meditation.

Some of my co-explorers in the early 1970's achieved the following results:

Choice	*Result*
Hands—cheeks	A romantic tenderness not previously expressed.
Lips—breasts—crotch	An actress created an unusual free-flowing movement.
Arms—chest	An actor created extremely interesting behavior with his partner in an improvisation. He created the illusion of physical contact.
Arms	A tall actor experienced a different physical sense. His classmates remarked that there was less self-consciousness regarding his height.
Nose—teeth	An actress achieved an exceptional centered strength and belief.
Network of veins	The actor entangled his partner in an imaginary net.

Recently, an actor in my workshop worked with this exercise and developed an unusual sense of a double in the space around him. The experience endowed him with an increased consciousness of his entire acting instrument.

THE OUTER SPATIAL OBJECTS EXERCISE

1. Select an action that you feel is particularly applicable for the nature of this exercise.

2. Select a choice or choices from the suggestion list that will fulfill your action's meaning:

Examples

To go with the flow: Eyes—lips—knees
To blunder: Lips—elbows—base of spine—knees
To demand recognition: Sexual organs—chest

Choice Suggestions

Pelvis—breasts	Dimples—nipples
Hips—pectoral—legs	Nerve network of body
Collar bone	Eyelashes as antennae
Lower half of body	Feet—teeth
Mouth—back—hips	Thighs—feet—hands
Dandruff scales	Lips
Thighs—chest	Spine
Back—hip area	Feet—arms
Eyes—feet—mouth	Crotch—breasts
Arms—eyes	Hands—fingers
Eyebrows—jaw—shoulders	Ears
Arms—chest	Lips—bust—crotch
Chest—mouth	Torso—leg network
Hips—breasts	Pelvis

Mouth—chin—cheeks

Pelvis—breast

Jaw—elbows—knees

Eyeballs—hands

Feet—thighs

Lower back—tongue

Writhing intestines

Anus—lips

Erect penis—eyes

Stinky feet and arm pits

Mid chest—knees

Throat—root center

Eyebrows—jaw

Hands—cheeks

Eyes—hands—mouth

Legs—solar plexus

Ear—nose

Heart—arms

Lungs

Clitoris—breasts

Navel—legs—eyelashes

Pubic hair

Lower abdomen—forehead

Sexual center—heart

Guidelines for the Outer Spatial Objects Exercise

...Create energetic sensations in the area(s) chosen or sense the basic energy in the area(s).

...When this exercise is done following a period of relaxation, the body is ready to permit energy to flow effortlessly. Sense yourself sending forth natural radiations and body frequencies—powerful faculties possessed by all fine performers. Permit the sensation to exist without activating any muscles in the chosen area(s).

...With a relaxed but energized feeling in the chosen area(s), you can more easily sense the energy of body parts drift into surrounding spaces. Use imaginative control in the manner in which you modulate the flow and stream— quickly, slowly, gradually, in spurts, etc. The controlling element should have relevance to the behavior you wish to create for your action.

...It is important that you not move the chosen area. You cannot physically send parts of your body into nearby or distant areas, but you can propel energy waves from specified parts. The body should be motionless as you effortlessly release the energy.

...While sitting or standing, project the energy into a nearby area and then gradually into farther areas. The energy flow of the exercise is not exclusively a frontal flow. If you are using the spine as a choice, propel the spine's energy into the space behind you. For example, an actress who permitted the energy of her eyes to go out through the back of her head remarked on the unusual kind of dimensional experience it created.

...Grant the energy of your chosen area(s) to be released in regular or irregular waves and patterns. The projection of energies can have different designs: a missile on course, zigzagged patterns, explosive bubbles, soft streams of feeling or uncontrollable frequencies. Consciously will the transference of these types of energies while maintaining contact with the elements which generate and control the energy flow.

...Connect with the force field around you when you walk. Sense the energy preceding you and drawing you toward the object of your attention, whether it is a person or another part of the environment.

Examples of the Outer Spatial Objects Combination Exercise

To beguile: OSO—Lips—neck—abdomen
Smell—Lavender
Sp. Obj.—Moonbeams

To inspire: OSO—Eyes—chest—thighs—soles of feet
Ch.Imp. Enthusiasm.
OA: Intense heat in genital area
PDA: Throat

To get someone in bed: OSO—Eyes—breasts—crotch
Sp. Obj.—Moonbeams

To challenge: OSO—Center of forehead, eyes, hands
Ch. Imp. Anger.
OA—Pounding in brain
PDA—Stomach

To find an open heart: OSO -Heart—throat
Taste—Copper
Cold syrup in stomach

To regain my masculinity: OSO—Heart extended out of chest
Ch.Imp.—Warmth
OA—Solar plexus
PDA—Arms and legs

To castigate: OSO—Heart
Sp. Obj.—Pounding fists
Aura—Orange: Neck and shoulders
Purple: Head and rest of body

To flirt: OSO—Eyes
        Ch. Imp. Tenderness.
        OA—Warmth in base of spine
        PDA—Base of head

To have a ball: OSO—Intestines
        Ch. Imp. Joy.
        OA—Head
        PDA—Legs
        Place—Visual

To worm out of trouble: OSO—Forehead—eyes—shoulders
                IMO—Electric sparks in arms and
                    fingers

To speak outright: OSO—Hands—tongue—lips
                Introjection of a person

INNER MOVING OBJECT EXERCISE

Lillian Gish, whose award winning film career has covered a span of nearly 80 years, is an actress of supreme talent and, assuredly, phenomenal career longevity! Her wisdom highly qualifies her to explain the rapport between the camera and the actor. She believes in the psychic strength of the camera lens to capture what is going on inside of an actor. She also gives testimony to the power of a motion picture camera, which like an X-ray, has an uncanny facility to peer into an actor's interior. For the actor, the Inner

Moving Object Exercise offers a rich inner substance that a camera (even a still one) is always eager to capture.

This exercise can offer an exciting adventure in acting technique as you sense your viscera surge with distinctively new energies. The result can be an increased sense of the pleasures in your inner space. Richard Selzer writes in his book, *Mortal Lessons: Notes on the Art of Surgery,* that we are denied the sight of internal organs. This exercise offers a means of internal visualization as you probe into your organs. Its purpose is to grant you a higher sensitization of inner qualities.

Stanislavski rebelled against the flailing of external parts with no inner reality. He developed means to create inner reality—which you have already experienced in the sensory exercises. The Inner Moving Object Exercise will enable you to contact force fields within and will invigorate you in a way far beyond the power of inner sensory exercises which focus on sharp pain, sharp taste and sharp smell.

The therapeutic nature of this exercise creates a direct means of changing your internal functions. Scientific experiments have revealed that the nervous system has a capacity for growth that is not fully appreciated. Experiments point out that the nervous system can even grow new fibers. At the world-renowned Menninger Foundation, individuals have been able to relieve their migraine headaches by warming up the inside of their hands. This is accomplished by sending mental messages along the nerve circuits that terminate in the many nerve endings of the hands. This is not unlike the manner in which you accomplish relaxation by sending mental messages to areas experiencing some degree of tension.

THE INNER MOVING OBJECT EXERCISE

1. Select an action.

2. Select an Inner Moving Object. The object can be as small as a thimble or coin, but preferably no larger than a tennis ball. It can also be a clump of energy—such as electricity—or it can be a ball of energy localized in the stomach to give it warmth. You can also miniaturize larger objects: animate objects such as a person or pet; inanimate objects such as telephones, musical instruments, or a compact disc player. The reason for miniaturizing an object is so that you can carefully track its movement inside of you.

Examples

Action	*Choice*
To attain focus	Mechanical spring
To keep my secret	Cluster of spiders
To free myself	Flame of candle
To shock them	Coiled rattlesnake
To share my power	Ice cube
To strike back	Door spring
To be in control of the situation	Diamond pin
To hold out	Circular saw
To have fun	Tape recorder

Choice Suggestions

Light bulb	Tear drop
Cement pole	Tapeworm
Sexual part	Ulcer
Bubbles	Taffy
Barbed wire	Sugar cane chopper
Sharp object	Icicle
Personal object	Fly
Merry-go-round	Greasy blob
Soggy cereal	Light beam
Erratic metronome	Razor blade
Lips	Glob of honey
Compression spring	Sandpaper
Fist	Baby rattle
Fire	Octopus
Soggy green moss	Scalpel
Molten lava	Glob of indigo
Cacti	Clump of rock music
Spinning top	Comet
Friendly pixie	Grandfather's clock
Sand paper block	Pinball
Thorn	Ball bearing
Opal in solar plexus	Gong
Amethyst	Lover's heart
Red hot coal	Camellia
Popping corn	Caterpillar

Liquid ball of battery acid	Spotlight
Boxing gloves	Ping-Pong ball

Guidelines for the Inner Moving Object Exercise

...Before allowing the object to move to different parts of your body, localize it in an area and define its shape. It can then move up and down inside of you—stopping, traveling a circuitous route, etc. Its routing will give rhythm and specific meaning to words, phrases and sentences in improvisational or memorized dialogue.

...The object can be transformed into an amoeba-sized object, if you wish, and yet have the capacity to stretch, amorphously disintegrate and come together again.

...Taste it when it travels through the stomach; when it passes through the nose, smell it; hear it in the ears; treasure it in the heart (or maybe even let it break your heart); let it shake up deep recesses in the pelvic area.

...The object moves around inside the body just as the Wandering Personal Object in *All About Method Acting* moved around on your outer surface.

...Let the object move into an area that resists it and then quickly expel it. As you oust it, question the need for you to reroute the object.

...Use your choice to discover the nature of sensitivities in the nerve network. This exercise can also effectively deal with any locked areas which often contain strong sensations. An object entering such a locked area can throw it open and create sensations with sudden spontaneity. So, if you have not successfully resolved locked-up areas, this exercise offers another opportunity.

...As a strong acting choice, I often describe the behavior that Jack Nicholson created in *One Flew Over the Cuckoo's Nest*. Most of you will vividly recall the scenes in which his character was subjected to shock therapy, his body writhing with the force of 10,000 watts that Nicholson imagined passing into his body. The Inner Moving Object is capable of creating such a force through an inventive and imaginative choice and your willingness to go with it.

I would like to relate a few of the unusual results I have seen students attain with this exercise:

An actor localized an object in his knees where he had pain for several days. His choice of a cluster of electrical energy totally relieved the pain. After completing the exercise, he showed an exuberance I had never seen as he realized that he could actually change, at will, bodily feelings and sensations.

An actress created a larger vocal range for the first time when she did the exercise. It took months of previous sensorial and beginning transpersonal exercises to reach this achievement.

An actress used an Inner Moving Object of a heart in her head area, and the expressions seen on her face captured the lively pulsations of a pumping heart.

An actor used a large gold nugget in his solar plexus. Its use became like a solar plexus battery that sends forth white light into the body.

After you have worked with a single object, you can then select two objects.

Examples

Action	*Choices*
To get on the good side	Diamond in head area
	Bubble in stomach
To mock everyone	Fly in head
	Moving ulcer in stomach
To bewitch	Phosphorescent indigo blob
	Cowrie shell
To shock them	Turned-on chain saw in head
	Razor blade traveling through muscle tissues
To guide	Spinning top in head
	Comet in veins
To make them laugh	Aluminum foil in head
	4th of July sparkler
To know no boundaries	Mercury
	I Ching Hexagram
To pester	Violin bow
	Glob of molasses
To prepare the earth	Ice cube in head
	Fireball—Lower part of body

You can also select one or two objects to use in combination with another choice.

Examples of the Inner Moving Object Combination Exercise

Action	*Choices*
To rip open delicate matters	IMO—Bubbling geyser Diamond Place—Visual
To emancipate	IMO—Small prayer scroll Sp. Obj.—Outer space creatures
To carry out an important mission	IMO—Electric coil current in torso Warm ball in throat Sex object in chest Cement poles in legs Taste—Chocolate
To trust myself	IMO—Nordic steamer in right brain Friendly pixies in left brain Sp. Obj.—Domesticated animals
To protect my dignity	IMO—Ice cube in head Ch.Imp.—Electricity in groin to chest and spinal area
To expand and dissolve	IMO—Ocean waves in chest Bird in right brain Sound— Music interrupted by air raid siren

PROJECTED SPATIAL OBJECT EXERCISE

Carl Jung had a mystical connection with material objects. While discussing poltergeists during one of his meetings with Sigmund Freud, he told Freud that a large cupboard would momentarily let out a cracking noise and when it did, Freud turned white. That may have been the beginning of Freud's gradual change in his beliefs about the psychic world. On another occasion, during talks with his longtime friend, Laurens van der Post, Jung warned about a recording machine with which van der Post had hoped to record Jung's spontaneous thoughts. Jung believed recording machines harbored animosity towards him and even if inanimate, could still be hostile. Jung's intuition went unheeded and nearly seventy hours of recording were damaged and lost forever. Jung had a strong belief that both animate and inanimate objects, as well as human beings, are joined through his famous theory of the collective unconscious.

In Yosemite, John Muir could spend an entire day studying a plant unknown to him. He attempted to establish an intimate interconnection with each new plant as a revealing source of insight about the species.

In the planetary village of Findhorn on the northern coast of Scotland, not far from the Arctic Circle, the residents have a strong belief in the spirits who dwell in their world-renowned gardens in which giant plants have grown under the most improbable circumstances. Deva spirits also inhabit their printing presses, stoves, enormous espresso equipment and an equally enormous dough machine. The machines and equipment are all given names and residents dwell upon affecting the energy of the machines in the same way that they meditate upon entering into the life of a plant. How often have you told a stalled automobile to "Please start up..." and sometimes had it respond to your request? Coincidence? Perhaps.

There are physicists who admit that their theories were first experienced on a mystical level of consciousness and believe that the material objects which surround us are not passive and inert, but have their own vibrating dynamics. (Pythagoras told his followers that a stone is frozen music and that every object has its own personality.) Notable scientists have predicted that humankind will someday be able to harness the dynamics of unseen universal energies.

Fritjof Capra's *The Tao of Physics* substantiates the belief of some of the world's renowned physicists that nothing is static in the universe. Instead, they believe that the universe is in a constant state of dynamic change since everything has a molecular structure of atoms that are constantly alive, vibrating and dancing. These beliefs relate to the realities of the fourth dimension that physicists and mystics seek.

Some people are inclined to scoff at the belief that inanimate objects have a life of their own. Nevertheless, the belief continues to be acknowledged in innumerable everyday occurrences. At Northern Illinois University, a psychologist-educator requested his electric shop students to relax and then told them to imagine being moving electrons inside of a hot wire, tripping down the wire's electrical coil while constantly coming into contact with other electrons. An instructor of a Chicago Cubs training program had his athletes stretch out on the floor. After a period of relaxation, he told them to get into the ball or bat and taste it, smell it, etc. On a different level, psychiatrists are using photographs to unlock patient psyches by asking the patient to transport themselves into the meaning of a photograph in much the same way that the standard Rorschach test has been diagnostically employed.

While vacationing on Kauai, I had an experience similar to that of the colorful character Don Juan in Castaneda's *Journey to Ixtlan*. In the book, Don Juan says that a sorcerer can focus on any object and find his way into and affect it. To prove it, Don Juan made a car inoperable by willfully getting inside the spark plugs. During my month's holiday on mystical Kauai, I rented a car and at the end of the rental period, I returned the car to Lihue, the island's capital. Lihue is about 21 miles away from the isolated cottage (rented from a kahuna) in which I stayed. The cottage is located at the end of Menehune Road near the entrance to the southern end of Waimea Canyon, often referred to as the Grand Canyon of the Pacific. After returning the car to Lihue, I had to hitchhike to Waimea since there was no public transportation on the island. I immediately got a ride from a teacher at a Kauai college who was able to take me to the Koloa intersection, about 15 miles from Waimea. It began to rain as I stood at the intersection, thumbing for a ride to Waimea. Hundreds of drivers ignored me during the hour I remained at the intersection. Finally, I started to walk towards Waimea, thumbing as I walked along side of the road—still being ignored by passing cars. Impulsively, I decided to test the power of the Projected Spatial Object Exercise by projecting energy into the brakes of the next car and willing the car to stop. I turned around and saw a red VW about 300 yards down the road. I gave myself to the moment, trusting that I might have the power to stop the VW. I concentrated on the vehicle and attempted to physically enter into the brakes with my consciousness. The VW stopped! The Kauaian native driver told me that the reason I had such bad luck at the Koloa intersection was because it is a favorite stopping place for Pele, the Hawaiian Goddess of Volcanoes, who travels through the islands and if she is in a temperamental mood, she can do a number on you. I prefer to think that Pele desired to convince me that there are mystical forces on her garden island.

My most profound experience with hidden forces occurred in West Berlin during a Christmas holiday workshop I conducted for acting students from various European countries. Shortly before leaving Los Angeles, I acquired a book of photographs Alfred Eisenstaedt had taken before his pre-World War II departure from West Berlin and upon his return to Berlin forty years later. In the book, he spoke of the Victoria-Luise Platz, which neighbored Theaterhaus where I conducted the workshop. He also mentioned living on a nearby street, which had been renamed Treuchtlinger Strasse, and that Albert Einstein lived across the street from him. At the time of his postwar return, there was still a plaque on Einstein's house. On a misty winter afternoon, I walked up and down the small street in a vain search for the house with the Einstein plaque. The buildings on the street were all modern, so apparently the remaining old houses had been demolished. I stood in the driveway between two apartment houses and attempted to imagine where on the street the Einstein house might have stood. At that very moment, a huge slab of stucco loosened itself from the sixth floor level of one of the two buildings and crashed in front of me, letting up a large cloud of dirt and stucco particles. Was this some kind of depiction of Einstein's world of atoms and molecules, I mused, informing me that his house had been located on

the very spot I was standing? Having a belief in the super-
natural (as did Stanislavski) I could only regard the occur-
rence as a transcendental pleasantry between myself and
the force of a great immortal mind.

Actors in my workshop, have also unleashed the kind
of mystical experience I have had with the essence of the
Projected Spatial Object Exercise. An actress practiced the
exercise at home and projected her consciousness into a
Melaleuca Linariifolia tree (commonly known as the Flax-
leaf Paperbark) in her garden. The tree thrives in harsh
conditions and sends forth fluffy white flowers. During her
practice, the actress had indeed entered into the tree's spirit.
She was convinced of this when she arose on a February
morning and beheld blooms on the tree, which she had
never known to flower until the month of June.

I hope you can relate to the beauty of her experience.
Maybe so, since we are becoming collectively more receptive to the parapsychic experiences of people from all walks
of life.

Theravada Buddhists of Tibet feel consumed by the
object upon which they concentrate. In 1988, visitors to New
York's Museum of Natural History were able to observe
Tibetan monks (now exiled in India) create the 500 B.C.
Kalachakra Mandala in sand. It is conceivable that wit-
nesses to this beautiful and sacred event were enlightened
by the manner in which the disciple monks arrived at the
center of their creation. Throughout the thirteen-day event,
the monks inhabited a space of spiritual value.

An actor should also know how to inhabit another space
and dissolve his/her ego, with the same spirit of Tibetan
monks, in order to inhabit the space of a character. The
Projected Spatial Object Exercise dwells upon this desirable
value.

THE PROJECTED SPATIAL OBJECT EXERCISE

Exercise One

1. Select an animate or inanimate object.

Choice Suggestions

Clock	A red cord
Screw driver	Starfish
Vase with flower	Pliers
Indian headdress	Paperweight
Electric fan	Candlestick
Ceramic bird	Incense burner
Box of nails	A burning candle
Kaleidoscope	Feather duster

2. Select an action.

Guidelines for the Projected Spatial Object Exercise

...Attempt to sense yourself entering into another dimension, as you transfer your consciousness to the interior of the object and capture the intrinsic nature which you imagine the object possesses. Endeavor to enter into the spirit of the object and charge it with your energy streams. Allow ego boundaries to dissolve as you become receptive to the object's essence, letting it absorb you so that you and the object are in conjunction.

...After getting to the very marrow of an object's nature, transport yourself beyond its spirit and mood. Create its form, textures and shape. Permit the object to become animated as you enter into its hidden dimensions. Tap into its energies. Give it commands as you pour energy waves into it and merge with it. Try to determine what it is about the object that causes internal and external changes.

Exercise Two

Select a picture, painting or photograph which depicts numerous details of lines, shapes and forms. I offer actors a large collection of full-page magazine drawings and photographs (sans commercial printing) of bold pictorial subject matter. There are usually richer complexities in a picture or painting than in an object because of varying colors and other details.

...Inhabit the picture and let it come to life in the same manner as you did with the object. An additional behavioral value can suddenly accrue from amidst the endless details. In experimenting with a possible behavioral choice for a character, be aware of the moments that have the precise value you are seeking. In a selection rich with behavioral possibilities, only certain experiential moments may offer you the specific qualities you wish.

...To fully realize your results in an improvisational or memorized scene, capture the intrinsic rhythm of the picture or painting as your imagination travels among the details. Establish the same rhythm in your walk, movements and gestures. Stanislavski said that an actor must find the rhythm of a character, cautioning that while a musician is given the rhythm by the composer's notes, an actor must find the notes in the playwright's writing.

...You may wish to refer to Joseph Campbell's *The Power of Myth* and his description of James Joyce's epiphanies in the chapter entitled "Masks of Eternity." Basically, epiphany means to take a commonplace object, place a frame around it, and dwell upon its various parts. Concentration is focused on how the parts relate to the whole and particularly the rhythm of this relationship.

...When an epiphany has been experienced, it can be similar to the flash of aesthetic insight that occurs in higher states of consciousness. I suggest that actors also use the "epiphany frame" to study portions of a picture or painting, especially in order to perceive details in greater depth and to capture the rhythm as the frame is moved about.

...Permit the picture or painting to affect you in such a way that you deeply feel its illuminating center. You can elevate the basic sensory place exercise to a much higher level by entering into your Projected Spatial Object and letting it take you to an unexperienced place of greater richness than places you have actually experienced. Be like the talented motion picture director David Lynch who gave up painting to become a film maker because he wanted "a painting to move." And you never know what career momentum can occur by immersing yourself into the dramatic heart of pictorial matter. You will recall how Jessica Lange was inspired to produce the movie *Country,* in which she also starred. She had been very moved by a newspaper photograph of a family being evicted from their farm. Her emotional involvement with the depicted event was so strong that she persuaded Sam Shepard to write the screen play.

Often in my workshop, there are actors who have traveled one of many spiritual paths, as do many young people in search of some meaning amidst rampant materialism. A spiritually disciplined actress said that she did not have to think in this exercise as she permitted her choice to think for her. Another student said he experienced the higher consciousness that he had sought during twelve years of meditational practice and never achieved. (However, I pointed out to him that perhaps his years of meditation had prepared him for his initial Projected Spatial Object Exercise.) The exercise gave him a heightened physical experience and awareness and he dealt with what was happening to him. Afterwards he said, "In years of meditation, I never had a charge like that. It was like volts of electricity going through me." The picture he chose from my collection was a picture of a space robot traveling through spaces of cosmic forces. Coincidentally, within a short time, he was hired to be a robot who walked down the aisle in the 1987-88 Academy Awards. And, today, I took time from making the final corrections on this portion of the book to search for misplaced reading glasses in my garage. I did not find the glasses, but I did find a miniature wind-up robot from a Christmas stocking of some years ago. As Shirley MacLaine has said: "Nothing is coincidental. I don't believe in coincidence...I believe in the merging of the physical and spiritual."

Other Projected Spatial Object Exercises

Combine a picture or object with sensory and/or transpersonal choices.

Example

To push my case

PSO—Yosemite cliff

IMO—Full moon in the head

An interesting challenge is to create an introjection and attempt to project the introjection's psyche into an object or picture.

PHYSIOLOGICAL AND PSYCHOLOGICAL FUNCTIONING EXERCISE

When I was preparing the first editions of this book, this exercise was in an early stage of experimentation. Since then, the exercise has evinced an ever-increasing usefulness for improving technique. It is an exercise which investigates and defines an individual's senses, anatomy and organs. The actor learns how activities of these parts of the body lead to emotions and physical presence. I have seen actors achieve remarkably new physical sensibilities and more impassioned feelings through this exercise.

The exercise enables the actor to communicate enormous inner power with any part of the body. The results enhance both inner inclinations and outer kinetic energy. Much of the kinetic energy that occurs is due to a sort of competition between organs.

One actor in my workshop reacted to readings about the exercise by suggesting that it seemed to be a repetition of sensory work—in which he had already had six years of training! I suggested that he take a stab at it anyway. We both acknowledged that the results of his first attempt were greater poise and an infinitely superior inner and outer expressiveness. The way he had previously employed sensory choices seemed to be like a barrelful of conventionalities when compared to the unique and lively details that he attained working with this exercise. Though he did not abandon the use of sensory choices, he discovered that he could use his training in a more imaginative and effective way. As he had been a pre-med student, the nature of the exercise may have awakened his understanding of the connections between the body and the physiological aspects of his acting instrument. He also discovered, as do all who do the exercise, that organs other than the sensory organs abound with their own special communicative powers.

This exercise can be used alone or in combination with other tools. The examples will convey how certain choices create behavioral nuances by developing, simultaneously, inner emotions and a new outer physical tone.

P.D. Ouspensky likened human beings to machines with centers that serve particular functions. John Toolan, in his engrossing book *Facing West from California Shores*, ranks the essence of this exercise foremost among many highly regarded human potential therapies and spiritual teachings. He points out that the philosophy of this exercise appears in Hinduism, Buddhism, the Kabballa of rabbinical theories and Eastern Orthodox Christianity.

Now and then, I have seen the exercise offer tremendous value changes to an actor who, for whatever reason, has not been able to achieve a well-sharpened acting image through other means. The following is an example of the choices and results I recently witnessed in the work of a developing actor.

Action: *To doubt their faithfulness*

Eyes: To see the world of epistles

Ears: To hear them speak of one's virtues

Mouth and stomach: To hunger for more sensitivity

Heart: To pump freedom through my veins

Thighs and arms: To hold up under the lies

The resulting battle between his inner and outer choices created an immensely interesting physical presence, a goal upon which we had been concentrating. The duality of his choices both drained and energized him. He also created an enormously rich emotional disturbance as powerful as a successful emotional memory exercise can attain and infinitely more artistic. One of the most expressive results was the concentration used to hold back tears welling up in his eyes.

The second time he did the exercise, he used the following:

Action: *To figure it out*

Ears: To hear gibberish

Eyes: To see everything in motion

Genitals: To feel isolation and dislike

Hands and feet: To reach out for compassion

The genital choice created intense inner pain and the gestures of his hands and feet were both introverted and outgoing. These expressive results were accompanied by stirring, sensitive emotions which contained sparks of anger.

The third time he did the exercise in combination with other choices.

Action: *To pull myself together*

Eyes: To see miles down the road

Ears: To hear approaching horses

Ch. Imp.—Increased sensitive heart beat to the shoulders and arms

(He also added narcissism to his character by using the sensory choices of smell for the head area and sun on the legs.)

For the first time, this actor created an energetic style that attested to his ability to work with classical material. His energy in the exercise combined a physical forward thrust with disorganized features. In addition, flashes of danger occurred in a cold but playful manner.

This talented actor discovered that this exercise can be an intellectual and artistic pursuit as manifested in his choices and results. It catapulted his work into another dimension and he attained a higher level of expressive freedom. For this actor, and perhaps for many others, the exclusive use of sensory choices had failed to create desirable physical results, leading to a dead-end for his undeveloped talents.

Guidelines for the Physiological and Psychological Functioning Exercise

...Above all, you must have complete and total faith in its possibilities for you.

...Put your consciousness into different areas. For example, do not consciously think about where to put your feet; with a choice for that area your consciousness is in your feet.

...Develop a sense of when you are on the mark with your choices so that you quickly become aware of when one of the choices goes off center.

...As part of your film technique, you can plan choices for the camera to capture your personal chemistry, particularly as reflected in your facial expressions.

...With your choices you can increase the range of your physical presence with knowledge of new techniques to generate tactile images.

...When you freely change your focus from one choice to another, you may discover a fresh kind of spontaneity in your work.

In using inner organs to communicate your actions, keep in mind that they have both spiritual and physical values.

The following list is taken from an interview printed in *Psychology Today* between Sam Keen and Oscar Ichazo of the Arica Institute. Ichazo who taught in Chile, embraced Gurdjieff and Sufi principles.

Ears perceive the meaning or logos and give us substance of things.

Eyes isolate forms.

The nose smells out possibilities.

The mouth and stomach sense our needs for nourishment.

The heart energizes the organism with its impulse.

The liver assimilates food and percepts we take into the organism.

The colon, anus, bladder and kidneys eliminate foods, ideas and experiences that are unmetabolizable.

The genitals reflect our orientation toward or away from life.

The thighs and upper arms reflect our capacity for strength.

The knees and elbows reflect the ease or awkwardness, the charisma with which we move through the world.

The calves and forearms are the means we use.

The hands and feet are used for going and taking, for reaching out for goals.

With my students, I have expanded the Arica Institute choices to make the exercise more useful for an actor's training. The following are choices made by my students.

Examples

To heal
Eyes: For soul searching
Heart: To feel
Hands and arms: To touch and hold true values
Feet and legs: To carry out a mission

To haul over the coals
Mouth: To savor the pain
Heart: To energize the anger
Stomach: To feel the guilt
Legs and feet: To reach my prey

To let it out
Eyes: To see the wonders of the world
Heart: To give energy
Hands and feet: To reach for fun things

To fantasize
Arms and hands: To exalt a dream
Heart: To traverse exotic lands
Genitalia: To relish caresses

To free myself from guilt
Ears: To hear negativity
Eyes: To seek reassurance
Thighs: To hide
Stomach and mouth: To release guilt

To tantalize
Ears: To hear dirty language
Nose: To smell out the possibilities
Heart: To glue courage
Thighs: To hide
Feet: To limit action

To be the devil's advocate
Eyes: To jam
Ears: To hear both sides
Mouth: To express confidence
Bowels: To eliminate unnecessary ideas
Feet and legs: To stand my ground

To rejoice
Eyes: To see joyful things
Ears: To hear exuberant sounds
Heart: For energizing the organism
Knees and elbows: For spontaneous expression

To cast off mediocrity
Mouth and throat: To taste forbidden potions
Spine: To absorb ocean waves
Hands: To shed drab colors
Feet: To skirt the mire

To get someone in bed
Eyes: To see sexual acts
Mouth: To taste sweets
Genitals: To fuel sexual excitement

To give myself
Eyes: To see auras
Nose: To smell the auras
Ears: To see the illusion
Mouth and digestive system: To eat nectar
Hair: To sense energy

To revenge myself on them all
Eyes: To see the horror
Ears: To hear discordant crying and screaming
Mouth: To taste bitterness
Nose: To smell out possibilities to do harm

To involve them in my experience
Ears: To hear a celebration
Eyes: To see the truth
Heart: To give power to the universe
Genitals: For frustration
Knees and elbows: For confidence

To reach my center
Spine: To hold it all together
Soles of feet: To connect with the earth
Eyes: As barriers to the soul
Throat: For expression

To please the world
Eyes: To search for kindness
Mouth and stomach: To sense disapproval
Hands: To show my affection and love

To live it up
Hair: To attract electricity
Ears: To hear laughter and sound of champagne glasses
Eyes: To see what I have never seen before
Thighs: To jump hurtles

To degrade
Eyes: To scrutinize pieces of pseudo-art
Body: To absorb distasteful elements
Hands: To take away their ego
Thighs and legs: To assert my stature
Nose: To smell their shortcomings

To run away
Ears: To hear the cries of sorrow
Eyes: To see the tyrants
Thighs and upper arms: To embrace and protect

To be on guard
Eyes: To isolate the truth
Ears: To hear positive sounds
Nose: To smell out good and bad possibilities
Stomach: To digest glass

To set on fire
Eyes: To see porno pictures
Nose: To smell out possibilities
Hands and feet: To carry forth opportunity
Genitals: To forge forward

To release my anger
Feet: For standing for what I am
Hands: To push and grab
Eyes: To see the truth
Stomach: To digest goodness and regurgitate poison

To make them acknowledge my presence
Hands: To create
Legs: To take me where I want to go
Smile: To mask insecurities

To find out the secret
Ears: To translate meanings
Eyes: To identify the center
Liver: To filter poisons
Thighs and upper arms: To maintain strength

To accuse
Eyes: To see their souls
Ears: To hear the lies
Heart: To pump the power
Arms: To keep them at a distance

To escape great danger
Ears: To pick up vibrations
Nose: To smell danger
Skin: To repel energy
Breath: To make me invisible
Genitals: To hold the possibility of life
Thighs and upper arms: To gather strength

To dominate everything
Eyes: To see things in miniature
Mouth: To taste control
Ears: To hear praise
Hands: To reach out and possess

To remain true to myself
Eyes: To see cars moving
Nose: Good smells
Mouth: Chew soft food, soft words, soft friends
Ears: Hear the silence of the dead
Heart: To energize my energies
Stomach: To reject food and accept liquid
Genitals: To desire and desist
Knees: For easy movement
Feet and hands: For reaching out and going forth

Physiological and Psychological Functioning Combination Examples

To prepare myself for love
Eyes: To see the good side
Hands: To touch the soul
Skin: To be tantalized
Stomach: To sense danger
Sound—Jazz music

To search for hidden clues
Ears: To listen for crucial evidence
Nose: To smell the problem
Sharp pain—Tooth
Ch. Imp.— OA—Roller coaster ride in stomach
            PDA—Eyes
OSO—Cheeks and knees

To nurture those around me
Hands: Reaching out to comfort others
Liver: To absorb unpleasant experiences of others
Colon and bladder: To eliminate those experiences
Ch. Imp.—Love. OA—Warm syrup in heart
            PDA—Head
Wandering Personal Object

To force connection
Nose: To smell out trouble
Elbows and knees: For charisma
Body: To absorb distasteful things
OSO—Eyes

To pierce and captivate the universe
Eyes: For penetration
Arms: For expression
Mouth: To entice
OSO—Legs

To guide
Heart: To pump the necessary stream of life
Thighs and upper arms: For the gift of life energy
Genitals: For enjoyment
Sp. Obj.—Sacred tablets

To rouse
Eyes: To perceive raging fire
Ears: To hear an intense driving sound
Mouth and stomach: To perceive hunger
Genitals: To sense pleasure
Feet: To make the earth tremble and go after goals
OSO—Eyes vibrating out through center of forehead

To flush them out
Eyes: To detect weakness or flaws
Body: To send out energy to them
Taste: Blood
IMO—Straight razor in digestive tract

To overcome my shortcomings
Heart: To reach out and touch
Eyes: To sort out good from bad
Brain—Electricity

To get to the heart of the matter
Circulatory system: To circulate beads of hope
Reproductive system: To give birth to discovery
Wandering Personal Object

To yearn feverishly
Mouth and stomach: To crave a ripe pear
Heart: To beat erratically
Hands and feet: To swim in rose petals
Overall—Cold mist
Stimulus—Dizziness

To rid myself of guilt
Eyes and ears: To see and hear cosmic realities
Heart: To pump the necessary stream of life
Introjection

To share my secret
Eyes: To see closed places
Ears: To hear a new sound
Nose: To take a chance
Heart: To give energy
Genitals: To fear rejection
Ch. Imp.—Nervousness. OA—Queasiness in stomach
                                    PDA—Eyes

To go past my limit
Eyes: To see myself crashing
Ears: To feel the echo of my pulse
Heart: To race out of control
Ch. Imp.— OA—Sensation in stomach
               PDA—Throat
Wandering Personal Object—Localized on chest and throat

To delve into my fantasies
Eyes: To see sexual acts
Ears: To hear contrasting sounds
Thighs and upper arms: To embrace and repel
Overall—Light spring rain

AURA EXERCISE

Numerous times during my years of study with the American Stanislavski disciples, I heard of their adoration of Eleanora Duse, an adoration they shared with Stanislavski. They gave detailed descriptions of her performances, but for some reason I do not recall any mention of the phenomena that some members of her audiences witnessed in the performances she gave during the last years of her life. It seemed to them as if she had created a "misty light" on stage. This was just one manifestation of the uncanny gifts that enabled her to create the mystical in acting. Another such gift was the power to speak in a whisper, yet be audible in the farthest reaches of a theatre.

The acceptance of concepts and ideas often depends upon whether they are scientifically provable. Sometimes even when scientific proof has been established, doubt can still linger. For example, many remain skeptical of faith healing even though the Menninger Foundation observed and documented the healing powers of such spiritual leaders as Rolling Thunder and Swami Rama. Scientists have confirmed the abilities of gifted clairvoyants to see auric colors around people. They have also, in the process, weeded out the charlatans.

Scientists using Kirlian photography at UCLA have established that roses, lizards, rocks, leaves, coins and all other objects—even the human body—radiate colors. Perhaps, you have seen the stunning Kirlian photographs of auras radiating from hands. Swami Muktananda (who had conversations with Astronaut Edgar Mitchell about his spiritual experience on the moon) after some persuasion by a Kirlian photographer, agreed to have one of his fingers photographed. What the photograph revealed was a circle of brilliant rays. Similarly, other researchers have seen pure colors captured on film when photographing the finger tips of healers. Some have even suggested that the auric field that surrounds a medical doctor gives benefit to the patient, and others have suggested that the doctor's aura may accomplish an actual cure. Yogis will point out that we can pass the energy of our chakras to another. This is the kind of communication that Stanislavski was investigating in his yogic prana ray emission experiments with actors.

Both science and religion give testimony to the presence of energies that emanate brilliant colors.

Certain contemporary physicists believe that light not only emanates from objects but that everything in the universe holds light, including the big bubble in which the universe itself resides. Colors are part of the natural phenomenon of light, and have been present since the beginning of time.

Both the Old and New Testaments give accounts of radiant white auras that surrounded Moses and Jesus when they returned from speaking to God. The dazzling white light that glowed from them was witnessed by their disciples and followers. During the era of the two biblical testaments, there was belief that the creator of the universe emanated a Great White Light. Bodily force fields are also depicted in Renaissance paintings as the halos surrounding saints.

The Los Angeles Times reported that a survey conducted in 1988 revealed that 47% of the journalism students at Columbia University believe in aura readings, even though many regard the practice as faddish. It is appropriate for student journalists to believe in the reading of auras, since journalists are often required to put into words what they feel vibrates from the people they encounter in search of a story. Positive features can be a warm disposition, a radiant smile, glistening eyes or an electrical presence. Negative personalities can convey dark colors, icy eyes or vibes that can give one the creeps. All of these qualities can be translated into colors. The actor, can consciously or unconsciously store such features in the memory for future characterization values.

Stanislavski experimented with an electrical wheel affixed with various colored light bulbs. He wanted to discover if actors could be emotionally affected by the spinning wheel of colors. In the final years of developing his System, his early experiments with lights were refined. At that time, he was exploring how the boldness or weakness of a color could relate to the energy of the physical activity of a character in a scene. His experiments may have been inspired by a combination of Pavlovian theories and the spiritually inclined theories of Wassily Kandinsky, the father of abstract art. Kandinsky, around the early part of the century, experimented with colors in painting to find out how they would arouse emotional reactions in the viewer.

Practitioners of holistic health apparently believe that colors do serve a purpose in healing. They have developed specific methods for breathing in colors to benefit both mind and body. Such a process is not much different from that used by some of Stanislavski's American disciples to arouse organic emotions through the value of colors.

More than 3,000 years ago, Chinese medicine divided the body's inner organs into five groups and specified how the colors of the organs relate to psychological functions. The deep yellow of the stomach stood for affection, while white brilliance of the lungs represented inspiration. For those of you who wish to pursue this topic, *The Yellow Emperor's Classic of Internal Medicine* (a publication of The University of California Press) provides a fascinating beginning.

The auric force field that surrounds the human body was investigated by the Swiss physician Paracelsus in the 16th Century, the physician Mesmer in the 17th Century and Wilhelm Reich in the present century. When Astronaut Mitchell discussed his interest in psychic phenomena and consciousness with Swami Muktananda, they were in agreement that the widespread acceptance of the auric field awaits the development of scientific instruments that will be able to prove the existence of the wide range of phenomena associated with colors, including the inner and outer light fields of the human body. It is conceivable that such instruments may yet be developed and will dispel the belief that auras belong to the world of the occult and esoteric. These instruments will substantiate the centuries-old knowledge that auras are really energy.

Two books that can help deepen your knowledge of colors, auras, force fields and energy transmissions are *Colour Meditation* by S. G. J. Ouseley and *The Luscher Color Test* by Dr. Max Luscher. The Ouseley book is a classic which can help you develop your color consciousness. Ouseley points out that our auras present the clue to our true character. The Luscher book is a guide that can reveal the true nature of your personality through your reactions to particular colors.

I have always given attention to which transpersonal exercises my students favor for creating behavioral values. Students seem to gravitate toward the Aura Exercise, revealing what is perhaps a natural instinct in actors to want to capture the energies present in life and art. A richly talented actor will radiate energetic colors; less expressive colors will be present in an actor lacking dramatic energy.

A brief description of color values is followed by the exercise examples. The examples will elaborate upon the colors that can be used to capture the meanings of actions and character types.

COLOR ATTRIBUTES

WHITE: Purity, unity, high spiritual devotion, ecstasy.

PURPLE: Power, greatness, honor, respect.

VIOLET: Holy, humility, reverence, sublimity, beauty, high spirituality, healing, art, mysticism.

BLUE: Truth, peace, faith, religious worship, meditation, loyalty.

INDIGO: Intelligence, integrity.

YELLOW: Intellectual seekers, self-discipline, desiring knowledge, laughter, optimistic.

GOLD: High spiritual color to calm.

PINK: Sympathy, compassion, love, gentle-
                 ness, sincerity, kindness, refined.

ORANGE: Intelligence, learning, assurance,
                 self-confidence, balance.

RED: Strength, respect, power, vitality,
                 love.

GREEN: Energy, hope, balance, youth,
                 health, success, pride.

INDIGO: Mystery, deep concentration, self-
                 understanding.

LAVENDER: High spiritual color.

The preceding list are colors associated with attributes.
Some darker colors tend to reveal negativity.

BROWN: Avarice

BLACK: Depraved

DARK GREEN: Jealousy

OLIVE: Deceit

DARK YELLOW: Suspicion

CLOUDY RED: Greed

Examples

To awaken
Green—Knees and elbows
White—Fingers and toes

To worm out of trouble
Olive green—Knees, elbows, fingers, toes, joints
Dark green—Mouth
Deep scarlet—Eyes

To make connection
Violet—Torso and heart
Gold—Shoulders, head, arms, wrists and hands

To stand above every one
Orange—Head
Red—Crotch
Green—Upper and lower body

To realize the Buddha in myself
Purple—Entire body
Blue—Stomach

To keep my eyes open
Pink—Heart
Indigo—Skin and hair

To never give an inch
Purple—Eyes and nose
Green—Chest and back
Red—Arms and legs

To save my soul
Murky orange—Heart, eyes, feet and voice

To be harum-skarum
Red—Different shades emanating from heart, brain and
lymph glands

To be a happy loon
Silver—Base of spine
Green—Spleen, hands and feet

To feel good about what I'm doing
Purple—Nervous system
Blue—Lungs and eyes
Yellow—Muscles

To seduce
Shades of red and black—Reproductive organs
Crimson—Eyes and mouth
Scarlet—Remainder of body

To be the center of attention
Gold—Muscular system
Violet—Extremities (including eyelids)

To enjoy my surroundings
Blue—Nervous system
Violet—Brain
Yellow—Legs

To haul over the coals
White—Head
Dark blue—Eyes
Burnt orange—Chest

To enlighten
Lavender—Eyes
Green—Lungs
Red—Abdomen

To seek comfort
Yellow—Nervous system
Pink—Heart
Red—Lungs
Silver—Toes and fingers
Green—Reproductive organs

To get back to a better time
Silver—Thyroid gland
Deep crimson shot with black—Heart

To break their will
Black—Head
Red—Eyes
Green—Cool green in hands
Blue—Legs

To draw the line
Head—Orange
Arms—Green

To win
White—Crown chakra
Green—Heart chakra

Examples of Aura Combination Exercise

To keep going
Blue—Face
Gold—Hair
Ch. Imp.—Laughter from throat into hands and fingers
IMO—Willow branches down spine and into arms

To captivate people
Blue—Eyes
White—Internal chest and lungs
Red—Genitals
Sound—A song

To know the difference
Orange—Skin
Pink—Skeleton
IMO—Laser beams

To ram it home unflinchingly
Purple and amber—Genitals
Sound—Saxophone
Place—Visual and smell

To mold
Cloudy reds—Eyes
Clear reds—Heart and stomach
Purple—Extremities
IMO—Erratic heart

To pick up the pieces
Yellow—Mouth
Sea blue—Breasts
Gray—Toes and feet
Black—Skin and hair
Ch. Imp.—Tightness from temples to eyes

To swim against
Pink—Upper body
Green—Lower body
Sp. Obj.—Spit balls

To stir up the moment
Red and orange—Head
Yellow—Body
IMO—Electrical coil

To proceed boldly
Blue—Head and arms
Green—Body and legs
P & P—Mouth to speak my mind
       Eyes to see the light

To burn my bridges
Crimson—Solar plexus
P & P—Eyes to see video violence
       Mouth to cultivate distaste

To needle
Fire truck red—Legs
Gold—Brain
Sound—Children's music and songs
Sp. Obj.—Massaging hands on upper body

To arrive at the last stop
Silver—Skeletal system
Green—Respiratory system
OSO—Eyes and extremities

To reveal a secret
White—Face and heart
Green—Body
Overall—Heavy humid air
OSO—Cheekbones and mouth

To remain on my feet
Yellow—Head
Purple—Torso and legs
Green—Arms and hands
Stimuli—Explosive feeling in head

To play it cool
Pale blue—Eyes
Gold—Hands
IMO—Glass fragments
Sp. Obj.—Popping hot grease
Visual—Slow motion movie sequence

Guidelines for the Aura Exercise

...As in the previous exercise, decide upon your action and, as with any new exercise, formulate an action that can lead you into more daring areas. During a scene, actions can assume new currents, just as colors can change in hue and intensity as the light shifts or the visual context alters.

...Think of the exercise as another opportunity for you to give more meaning to the space that surrounds you. Exercises that prepare you for the particular sensitivity of this exercise are the Outer Spatial Object Exercise, the Projected Spatial Object and the Physiological and Psychological Functioning Exercise.

...A prime concern in your experimentation with this exercise should be the illumination of the space around you. This is a quality for which any performer should strive. The exercise can offer you the means to grant a palpability to the space you illuminate. Early in his career, the rock star Sting, is said to have developed a visceral aura which intimidated and even frightened people. Later, his aura changed when he began to align himself with humanitarian concerns.

...During the exercise, try to maneuver and guide your auric energy. Verify that you are not a hit-or-miss actor, but can be right on target with the energy you emit. Believe that your acting instrument can create auric energies with a mysteriously powerful vitality. Sometimes the vitality of a person is so strong that we mysteriously sense the person's aura after he or she has departed. You can leave a lasting impression with casting directors by stimulating inner and outer colors.

...A highly refined type of concentration can be developed in this exercise as you surround yourself with a light which nothing can disturb. You develop a glowing, relaxed presence in any professional or personal situation. Manipulation of the aura is another way of enhancing your presence for communication with a receptive audience or of protecting yourself against disruptive elements in a hostile environment.

...Some have postulated that our auric energy extends an inch beyond our bodies and provides us with a private place. You might think of this if you use the Aura Exercise in conjunction with the Private Moment Exercise described in *All About Method Acting*. Others feel that our auric energy can radiate for a distance of up to 24 inches from our bodies. In film acting, the exercise can be helpful in creating expressive behavior within the confines of close-up shots.

...Since particular colors are associated with the inner organs, you can internalize a color with the use of choices for certain areas. A sense of red burning and fiery coals in the solar plexus can create a simmering inner aura, which can be maneuvered into a Channeling Impulse. You can also permit an aura to stream outward as an Outer Spatial Object.

...Invent colors for yourself, colors that you may not think exist in you. In creating a character, Olivier said that he paints a portrait of the character in his mind.

BRAIN EXERCISE

Over the past 30 years, researchers have made amazing discoveries about the functioning and the capacities of the human brain. Little by little we are learning about the powers of the endogenous drugs released within the brain to lessen pain, enhance or eradicate memories, and heighten or weaken the functioning of the remainder of the body. As neurologists, chemists, pathologists, and physicians unravel the mysteries of the delicate chemical balance required for physical and mental well-being, they are progressing toward the day when the imbalances that cause an array of disorders from stuttering to schizophrenia can be corrected artificially.

Much remains to be discovered about the three-pound, pinkish-gray object we carry about on our shoulders every day. Many of its secrets may never be unlocked. Actors however, can make use of the growing body of knowledge about the brain to use this powerful organ to create behavior.

The purpose of the Brain Exercise is to help actors discover how the brain, as an integral part of the acting instrument, can be used most effectively. The actor has as much prerogative as the scientist to explore such a vital part of the human body. The exercise will permit you to immerse yourself into a moment of creativity through a heightened awareness of the complex determinants of the brain's functioning.

Although some of you might not choose to keep the exercise as an acting choice, you will, nevertheless, gain greater knowledge of how your brain can create behavior.

In 1973, some of my first acting students helped me in the development of an exercise to use the brain as a creative force in acting. In 1977, a student who had studied with me for the longest period of time brought me a newspaper article about right brain theories and their use in the development of creativity. He proudly exclaimed, "We were right all along!" The Brain Exercise originally set off alarm bells in some circles, perhaps awakening fear of the kind of disturbances that had been caused by the misuse of the emotional memory exercise. After 15 years of working with the Brain Exercise, I have no doubt that it can be used to create behavior without any dangerous aftereffects.

The theories of right and left brain specialization continue to be controversial, particularly among some psychiatrists and psychoanalysts who doubt their validity. When information about hemispheric functioning moved from the scientific research front to the popular literature, many saw it as a passing fad. However, benefits are still being derived from research on the control centers in the distinct hemispheres of the brain. Opponents attack such research on the grounds that the brain functions as a harmonious whole and that no kind of human activity can take place without both hemispheres functioning.

The Brain Exercise in this book acknowledges that the whole brain is involved in acting. It gives the actor a specific way to use the knowledge that we have about the brain. Some of this knowledge is recent, while some of it has been known for centuries. Hippocrates, in 500 B.C., postulated how an injury to the right hemisphere could cause paralysis on the left side of the body; the Sufis, 700 years ago, delved into the characteristics of the brain's two hemispheres. The understanding of right brain specialization dates back over 1,000 years, when it began to be used in certain meditation and yoga techniques. It is only recently that attempts have been made to penetrate deeper into these venerable discoveries.

The brain contains 10 to 15 million neurons (at last count). It has the capacity to store nearly 100 billion items of information. Scientists can specify areas of the brain that have to do with our emotions and various sensations, but as far as they know nearly two-thirds of the brain is unused gray matter. Within this uncommitted region may reside the potential for realizing the as yet untapped powers of the brain.

We constantly hear discussion of the possibility of advanced intelligent beings existing elsewhere in the universe. Perhaps, before we can communicate with them and hear what they have to say, we will have to develop those areas of gray matter. Hologram researchers say that the entire universe resides within us. The holographic experience is one in which a person can enter into different consciousness when, in a brief moment, intuitive insight occurs. These researchers suggest that our hidden potentials may enable us to study higher beings and even converse with them. They believe that we have the ability to travel to cosmic spaces via the brain and then return to planet earth with new information for humankind's benefit. To accomplish this feat, we will need to use more than the usual twenty percent of our intelligence. While communicating with extra-terrestrials may sound like science fiction, serious-minded people do feel that it is possible to transcend our brain's present limitations. Perhaps these limits are transcended in each brief moment of intuition. Insights have a way of occurring during the most mundane daily activities—shaving, cleaning house or sitting on the upper deck of a bus.

In preparation for this exercise, it might be helpful to have a more accurate and detailed image of the brain, rather than viewing it as just a jelly-like mass. It could be useful to study some of the detailed illustrations of the brain and its various parts that can be found in numerous books. View the brain as a computer with complex circuitry or as a central switchboard with billions of nerve threads which telegraph an untold number of commands. Try to visualize the electrical activity in different areas—such as the hippocampus—and imagine using electrical impulses of neurotransmitters to create new behavioral experiences as commands are fired into any part of the body.

During your research, you will learn about the functions of both the left and right side of the brain. You will find out, if you weren't already aware, that many of our technical accomplishments are attributable to the left side of the brain which houses verbal ability and analytical, logical properties. Extreme right-brain dominance can sometimes render the individual unable to communicate verbally in an intelligible manner. Some brain theorists have said that words are not within the domain of the emotional right hemisphere, but belong in the logical left hemisphere.

Actually, the two hemispheres give each other support. This concept is reflected in Einstein's description of his mental functioning as being "combinatory play." Skillful balancing of both sides of the brain was demonstrated by many individuals during the Golden Age of Greece and the Renaissance. The right brain may have been dominant during the highly and uniquely creative historical periods mentioned, but surely the inventions of DaVinci and the art of Michaelangelo were not realized without the help of the left hemisphere.

Julian Jaynes has eloquently reasoned in his conception of the bicameral mind that the attributes of the right hemisphere of the brain will help us out of the quagmire in which the world finds itself. Nevertheless, his theories do emphasize the need to integrate the two hemispheres if we are to function in a superior way. This combination of the artistic right brain and the intellectual left brain is also found in such well-known artists as Leonard Bernstein, Martha Graham, John Cage, Eugene O'Neill, Wassily Kandinsky, Leonardo da Vinci and innumerable others.

The duality of human nature is attributable to the brain's two hemispheres. Some of the information from experiments with the hemispheres has disclosed interesting facts about forms of artistic functioning. Experiments with musicians, for example, point out that the right hemisphere responds more keenly to music. Studies concerning the character of the two hemispheres of the brain describe the functioning of the two spheres as follows:

The right side of the brain controls the left side of the body. It dominates in intuitive and nonlinear types of thinking. Its main functions, according to Robert Ornstein, seem to be related to orienting ourselves in space, realizing artistic talents, maintaining awareness of our bodies and recognizing faces. The recognition of shapes and textures, and powers of intuition are among its other attributes. It is considered the area of spirituality and holism. Music, art and imagination are dominant. It is regarded as the female side.

The left side of the brain controls the right side of the body. It dominates in analytic and linear type of thinking. It is the sphere of language abilities and mathematics. As emotional values are not as present in the left brain hemisphere, it is regarded as our cool side compared to the warm, emotional right side. It is regarded as the male side.

Early brain research in the mid-19th century revealed that any injury to the left side of the brain would result in language difficulties. Recently in this century, it was concluded that the right side was crucial for visual functioning. Discoveries accelerated rapidly in the 1960's and 1970's. One of the most notable results of brain research was the improvement of intellectual abilities with increased right brain activity. However, a most startling and controversial development occurred at Johns Hopkins University. Neurosurgeons performed surgical removal of the left brain without patients losing their verbal and logical abilities. If it was not a miracle, the neurosurgeons concluded, then the only remaining possibility was that the two spheres of the brain pass information to each other and that information from the left brain was already planted in the right brain before the revolutionary surgical procedure. This gives credence to the theory that the two hemispheres support each other.

I believe that the Brain Exercise emphasizes that the muscles of the brain are as important as the muscles of the actor's sensory equipment. When the actor develops a sense of powerful neuron forces passing into the right and left side of the body, creating a rich dichotomous form, he or she is no longer in the domain of the basic sensory exercises. The results I have see confirm that this exercise can achieve remarkable complex behavior.

In my workshop I am sometimes rewarded with the presence of sensitive talents with an artistic urge to explore their acting instruments to their fullest potential One such person was an actress to whom I assigned exploratory work for a scene. I requested that she use the Brain Exercise with a character type and physical objects. She made the following choices:

Action: *To investigate*

Character Type: Suspicious

Choices: Left Brain: Channeling Impulse. Mistrust. Pulsating Sensation to right side of the body

Right Brain: Channeling Impulse. Ardor. Sun to left side of body

Inner Moving Object— Personal object in uterus

In the exercise, she handled a suitcase filled with the bust of a woman, a scarf, and a book. The result was revelatory. While the left side of the body handled the objects in a free-flowing manner, the right approached them with a grasping stillness. The actress felt that she would not have accomplished these rich choreographic movements of the objects if she had not been focusing on the creative complexities of the Brain Exercise. The results far outstripped any I have seen when actors have used physical actions exclusively to work with objects.

The exercise demands a special kind of concentration from the actor. It can be an additional behavioral tool in an actor's arsenal and very useful when other choices are not successful. The farther reaches of acting in the System are beyond the images which the eyes see; the sounds which penetrate the ears; the sensations happening on the tongue; or aromas drifting into the nose. Through the transpersonal experiences offered by previous exercises in this book your acting instrument has gained the maturity needed to explore the brain's recesses.

Guidelines for the Brain Exercise

1. Select an action.
2. Study the following choices to gain an understanding of the exercise.

Examples

To show my true color
R to L: Open emotion and intuition
L to R: To control and block emotion with logic

To boist
R to L: Mountain stream
L to R: Petrified wood

To tell the whole truth
R to L: As if I were a child.
L to R: As if I were accosted by the police in the dark.

To throw it all to the wind
R to L: Drug rush
L to R: Hit and run car accident

To contradict myself
R to L: As if I were home at Christmas.
L to R: The excitement at the finish of a horse race

To cool them off
R to L: Desert warmth
L to R: Chill from Arctic ice

To do what I have to do
R to L: Explore possibilities
L to R: To go with impulses

To go as far as I can go
R to L: Music
L to R: Sharp spears

To discover the inner truth
R to L: Liquid
L to R: Graphic grid

To see it through to the end
R to L: Pleasant weather
L to R: Rain into thunderstorm

To seduce
R to L: Waterfall
L to R: 4th of July Sparklers

To try to do something
R to L: Fireworks
L to R: Money being counted

To confront the fear and let go
R to L: Pure energy of intuitive voice
L to R: Judgmental voices

To lust after her
R to L: Female
L to R: Male

Examples of The Brain Exercise Combination

To map uncharted territory
R to L: Warm, rising tub water
L to R: Visual of factory machine lathe
Visualization of turning point in four conversations

To brighten the atmosphere
R to L: Hundreds of laughing voices
L to R: Bright golden light
Sp.Obj—Hands touching me

To free myself
R to L: Growing roots
L to R: Slabs of granite
Overall—Cool mist

To lust
R to L: Fox to muscles, nerves and organs of the body
L to R: Very slow count to right thigh
IMO—Snake which turns into an OSO
Ch. Imp.—Desire from vagina to right hand

To worm out of trouble
R to L: Moon
L to R: Sun
Sp. Obj.—Slimy walls pushing in
As if I'm sitting in a crowded bus on a hot day with no
sleep.

To keep them off balance
R to L: Flower petals floating down like snow
L to R: Intermittent electrical charge
Ch. Imp.—Excitement. Burning hot fluid from bottom of
feet to spine and base of skull

To make them acknowledge my presence
R to L: Champagne bubbles
L to R: Obnoxious laughter
Sp. Obj.—Intermittent globs of corn starch

To joke with them
R to L: Chasing the dragon high
L to R: God and the devil in a sword fight
Sp.Obj.—Different pieces of a brilliant brain

Other Choices

Right Brain to Left Side of Body
Maternal
Moon
Alpha waves
Music
Wet kisses
Desire for sex and intoxication
Meadow
Rain forest
Overattachment to sensual pleasure
A kitten
Squirt of water

Left Brain to Right Side of Body
Paternal
Sun
Against intuition
Multiplication tables
Shooting rifles
Mental life of a stockbroker
Philosophical juggling
Spin cycle of a washing machine
Sunrise
Loaded gun
Flaming ball
Banging metal sound
Macho dictator

Guidelines for the Brain Exercise

...Recognize the enormity of unused resources in the brain's uncommitted gray matter and develop a strong belief in your power to stimulate that area. The gray matter exists in both the left and right brain.

...With your imagination, will the brain to do anything you wish it to do. This process involves "tricking" the brain.

...Look forward to accomplishing this exercise. The exercise can reward you with a feeling of being entirely dedicated to your creative power.

...Get a sense of the particular kind of functioning that the brain has. Know that it is ruling, guiding, talking to you at all times. The brain functions by communicating to the nerve cells in your body's massive, entangled circuits.

...Feel the energy from the brain sweep through the body and open various inner channels as if electrical switches were being turned on.

...Regard the brain as a gigantic electrical switchboard from which you can operate as you send messages from the brain into the body like electrical volts.

...Know that messages from the brain go into your spinal chord and nervous system. Get a sense of more of the brain's energy being needed to operate smaller muscles and less for larger muscles. Sense electrical brain currents moving into the arms and legs, up and down the right and left side of the body, into the hands and feet, and into the muscles of the face.

...Appreciate the exquisite and awesome nature of this mysterious and superior organ and your power to feed it suggestions to which it responds with breathtaking accuracy.

Marilyn Ferguson said in her book *The Brain Revolution: The Frontiers of Mind Research*, "We already have the superbrain. We have had it all along. That's what the brain revolution is all about."

HIGHLIGHT EXERCISE

> *You have to upset yourself. Unless you do, you cannot act. And there comes a time in one's life when you don't want to do it anymore. You know a scene is coming where you'll have to cry and scream and all those things, and it's always bothering you, always eating away at you and you can't just walk through it...it would be really disrespectful not to try to do your best.*
> Marlon Brando

A most impressive feature in an actor's talent is the emotional strength tapped during a scene which requires combustible behavior. A powerful acting instrument possesses the skill and creativity to achieve high states of emotion through behavior, capturing images and feelings that burn into the memory of an audience.

Intense emotions must be convincing or they can seem bombastic or semi-faked. Only a gifted and well-trained talent can use all of its resources to take emotional moments to the very edge.

This exercise is intended to give you keener insight into the vast resources of your emotional equipment. It offers a way to abandon yourself as you tap into deeper layers of your nerves and sinews; to shift your emotions into high gear and stretch to your limits without being hesitant or afraid; to test your commitment to acting through your willingness to go over the top.

Our day-to-day existence does not require us to know all of the facets of our true essence. In acting, you cannot completely know a character unless you have explored all sides of that character. This exercise requires you to pinpoint the polarities of a character and maintain a percussion-like counteraction between them. For example, feeling an element of trust in the midst of suspicion; maintaining a spark of hope during a time of fear; being elated about winning a coveted role yet having sympathy for the misery of a friend who lost out; or maintaining high moral and ethical values in public while abusing one's family members in private.

In the last century, Francois Delsarte taught acting and singing. He began as a singer, but faulty training botched his voice. Unfortunately, he turned to discovering principles of dramatic expression which in turn damaged the evolution of modern acting. Well-known actors studied with Delsarte and thereby helped to promulgate his superficial theories. He devised a series of gestures which imitated the external manifestation of emotion. He believed these gestures reflected universal reactions to various stimuli. By doing so, he fostered a popular approach to enacting an emotion in a direct way. As we know, Stanislavski rebelled against this cookie-cutter view of acting.

This exercise is an expansion of the characterization chapter in *All About Method Acting*. Carl Jung postulated that we experience the world in four ways: sensation, thinking, feeling and intuition. Though Jung thought it was possible to classify people into one of these types, he acknowledged that we each have the capacity to experience life in any of these ways. This capacity leads to the contradictions in a character which give a role its humanity and its inner state of flux. Opposing psychological values add rich dimensions to a role.

According to Jung, emotion consists of, first, the conscious perception of a stimulus, and, second, the corresponding physical manifestation triggered by the stimulus. For example, the emotion of fear can be triggered by the stimuli accompanying a moment of imminent danger. The corresponding manifestation might be a scream, cold sweat, rapid heart beat, etc. Even after the danger has passed, the aftereffects can still persist as shaking knees or a queasy stomach. Some psychologists disagree about which happens first: the conscious perception or the corresponding physical manifestation.

In this exercise, you may first elect to work with a single emotion. Thereafter, you will select choices which will capture separate emotions triggered by different stimuli. The amalgamation of different values will add dimensions to your character's behavior. It will capture that strange yet common experience of suddenly feeling an incongruous emotion in the midst of an overwhelming primary emotion.

Your effectiveness in a scene demanding a high state of emotion depends on your instinctive and intuitive ability to mix the traits of Jungian psychological types while at the same time balancing the conscious perception of a stimulus and its corresponding manifestation. This may strike you as intellectual mumbo jumbo, but your choices, as suggested by the examples, will automatically accomplish this for you without intellectual analysis.

The ability to create a highly emotional moment, or to sustain a powerful behavioral state, is frequently the determining factor in casting. A director will often select the most challenging moment in a role to find out if an actor will be able to handle the challenge with conviction and imagination. When confronted with such a casting situation or in giving an actual performance, the actor must know how much energy to use. Too much energy can mar a reading, audition or performance. In this exercise, you will experiment to determine the amount of energy you need for powerful moments.

In a workshop situation, try not to be concerned with being obvious or going overboard with the exercise. If you have never worked with extreme emotional moments, you will correct that omission and discover your ability to push yourself to emotional limits. Numerous fine actors who work in the somewhat restrictive confines of film feel compelled to return to stage work which affords them the opportunity to sustain a peak performance for a number of hours. On stage, they sense a much more intense involvement with their craft.

Guidelines for the Highlight Exercise

1. Select an action. Your action should not be related to a single emotion but, as in any combination, the action should suggest an emotional mixture.

2. Select a choice from either two or three of the following Highlight Exercise categories. Each category comprises a range of experiences so that you can be precise about the emotional content of your

selections. For example, you might select the experience of joyous in category number one as a stronger choice than contentment.

3. Select the technique choices to create the behavioral language of your selection from the following categories.

Category Listing

1. JOYOUS
   TRIUMPHANT
   BLISS
   CONTENTMENT
   HOPEFUL
   TRANQUIL
   STUDIED CONTROL

2. DISGUST
   DISTASTEFUL
   TURNED-OFF
   UPTIGHT
   ANNOYANCE
   EMBARRASSMENT
   IRRITATION
   RESTLESSNESS

3. TURNED-ON
   UNCONTROLLABLE LAUGHTER
   ORGASM

DRUNK

HIGH ELATION

HORNY

VOLUPTUOUSNESS

SENSUAL

4. PAIN

MENTAL SUFFERING

HUMILIATION

HIGH STRUNG

INSENSIBLE STUPOR

DISBELIEF

CONFUSED

5. SUSPICIOUS

HIGHLY CAUTIOUS

CURIOSITY

6. SORROW

BROKEN-HEARTED

DISAPPOINTMENT

LAMENT

REPENTANT

DESPONDENT

HOPELESSNESS

SUPPLICATION

FRUSTRATION

7. VINDICTIVENESS

ANGER

MURDEROUS RAGE
HOSTILITY
BITTERNESS
SPITEFULNESS
CRUELTY
OUTSPOKEN
SUPERIORITY
SARCASTIC

8. WEAKNESS
FATIGUE
WEARISOME
SUBMISSION
RELIEF

9. WORRY
FEAR
PANIC
ANXIOUS
COWARDICE
SHY
FRANTIC

10. HATE
UNCONCERN
REPULSIVENESS
ILL-MANNERED
INDIFFERENCE

11. TRUST
    SYMPATHETIC
    GIVING
    CONCERN
    GRATEFULNESS
    RESPECTFULNESS
    REVERENCE
12. SUFFOCATION
    STARVATION
    EXTREME THIRST
    SUNSTROKE
    HEART ATTACK
    NERVOUS BREAKDOWN
    AMNESIA
    SHELL-SHOCK
    CLAUSTROPHOBIA
    BREATHLESSNESS
13. SEXUAL LONGING
    SEXUAL FRUSTRATION
    AFFECTION
    ATTRACTION
    LONELINESS
    REJECTION
    INFERIORITY FEELINGS

...The exercise is not linear. When you are working with two or more emotions, do not create the first emotion and then discontinue it when you add the second or third emotion. One choice builds upon another. Their merging renders different values at different moments.

...It is important that you gauge the relative levels of energy you put into emotional selections. Since all of your selections are relevant to your results, do not permit one emotion to be victorious over another; instead maintain an interplay between them.

...Abandon yourself without concern about being "hammy." Being a ham is an occupational fringe benefit for some actors. Jean Stapleton delights in being hammy to the pleasure of her abiding audience.

...Permit the emotional choices to bristle with colors. Think of paintings or even clothing fabrics in which wildly divergent colors create a unity without reciprocity.

...Some have benefited from an increased ability to pinpoint the opposites necessary for combinations.

...Try to develop a sense of riding a peak emotional moment with ease. Like any demanding undertaking, this exercise will get your adrenalin going and may lead to a sense of fulfillment.

...Sometimes in the middle of a highlight you may sound one note that can have a shattering effect on an audience. Eric Clapton relates that he wishes to be able to make an audience cry on a single note. In the middle of a musical number, he seeks that moment when he can create a single sound that will make his audience "quiver with emotion." I'm sure that you can recall performances when the entire spectrum of an actor's craft suddenly clicked into place and you were carried away in a heart-rending or hair-raising or uproarious moment.

Examples

To be a loaded gun
Annoyance: Sp. Obj.—Insects
Disappointment: Personalization
Highly Cautious: Sound—Siren
                    Animal trait—Eyes of a cat

To assert myself
Panic: IMO—Tarantula in head
       IMO—Invading virus in body
Extreme Concern: Ch. Imp.— Energetic white light in
                            stomach to head

To be at my wit's end
Uptight: Ch. Imp.—Knife in groin to toes
Suffocation: Ch. Imp.—Boiling lava in stomach to mouth
Murderous Rage: Aura— Red in eyes, teeth and jaw
                            Electrical volts throughout the
                            body

To escape from a confining situation
Panic: Sound and visual of a place
Breathlessness: As if my lungs were filling with water.
Loneliness: Overall—Moonlight
Vulnerable: Animal trait—A caged cat

To put myself on the line
Repulsive: Stimulus of skin crawling
Spitefulness: Sp. Obj.—Spiders
Horny: Wandering Personal Object (localized in crotch)

To tell it like it is
Sympathetic: Sp. Obj.—Duplicated person
              Aura: White—Entire body
                    Pink—Hands
Disgust: Sp. Obj.—Another duplicated person
          Aura: Red—Body
                Gray—Hands

To drive them up the wall
Good spirits: Sp. Obj.—Bubbles bursting amid sparklers
Self-pity: Place—Visual
           Smell—Coffee cake baking

To avoid the issue
Optimism: Aura—Blue from top of the head
Dread: Ch. Imp.—Queasy stomach to eyes

To find my bearings
Disbelief: Place—Visual
Breathlessness: Ch. Imp.—Sensation in throat to heart
Affection: Overall—Sunshine

To protect a friend
Sympathy: Aura— Lavender in legs
                       Green in rest of the body
Hostility: OSO -Teeth
Anxiety: As if I was stuck in traffic.

To be the life of the party
Outspoken: Introjection
                  Ch. Imp.—Arrows in chest to sinus
Narcissistic: Sp. Obj.—Video screens
Affectionate: Aura—Yellow
               P&P—Thighs to hustle
                   Body alive with telling details

To stop the ugly rumors now
Suspicious: Place—Visual
Extreme Anger: Hot fire in gut
                  Sound of war drums
Trust: OSO—Hands
            Thighs

To gross them out
Uncontrollable Laughter: Sp. Obj.—Hands
Outspoken: Introjection

To live in the moment
Outspoken: Introjection and introject's Inner Monologue
Annoyance: Sp Obj.—Fleas
Respectful: Wandering Personal Object
Sensual: Heat—Localized on face

To hold onto someone
Extreme Disbelief: IMO—Ball of heat in body
                    Sound—Freeway in head
Betrayed: Substitutional Situation

To placate
Highly Cautious: Sp. Obj.—Naked Samurai blades
Totally Immoral: Overall—Fingers massaging entire body
                  Sound—Sitar music in the distance

To ventilate the problem
Jealousy: P&P—Hands to grab what's mine
              Eyes to see things the way I want them
              to be
Anger: Aura—Red in the eyes
       IMO—Hot spike
       Pain—Spine

To get ready to do battle
Organized: OSO—Eyes
          Smell—Roses
          Sound—Electrical calculator
Nervous Stimulation: Ch. Imp.— Electric current in feet to
                                stomach
                    Stimuli—Perspiring hands

To be in two different worlds
High Strung: Aura—Black
            Sp.Obj.—Infectious people
Studied Control: Pain—Headache
                 Personal Object
                 Sound—Metronome

To win at any cost
Uncontrollable Laughter: Ch. Imp.— Electricity in feet into
                                    entire body
Suspicious: IMO—Chess game in head
               Bees in blood stream
           Sound—Whispers
Hate: OSO—Stomach
     Sp. Obj.—Diamonds

To seek the truth
Disgust: Aura—Red
          Taste—Sour milk
Restlessness: Ch. Imp.— Ice water in bloodstream of feet to
                              head
Introjection

To capture the moment
Joyous: Ch. Imp.—Bubbles from chest to eyes
Reverence: Sound—Two songs
          Stimuli—Stomach queasiness
Curiosity— As if I were a child trying to open a Jack-in-the-
          Box without Jack popping out.

APPENDIX

Relaxation Exercise

The relaxation field already exists in you. The exercise is a time of self-affirmation, a time to love yourself and a time to know your uniqueness. Have an amiable encounter with yourself and tell yourself that your talent is unique. Give yourself this feedback at regular intervals throughout the exercise.

In a standing position, sense a draining of energy in all your physical and mental areas. Physical areas are the neck, shoulders, torso, arms, hands, pelvic area, legs and feet. Mental areas are the temples, brow, bridge of the nose, eyelids, eyeballs, optic nerves, the temple-nerves at the side of the eyes, scalp, cheeks, jaw and mouth.

Be aware of visually seizing on any objects around you. Avoid any sharp focusing. The eyes should not blink or flutter during the entire exercise. The lids are very active and alert during our daily activities. If the eyes tend to blink at any time during the exercise, it is best to gently close the lids because blinking can only perpetuate more blinking. By closing the lids, you can perhaps deal more effectively with the eyeballs and optic nerves, which may be causing some of the blinking. Blinking can also be caused by thinking about the exercise.

The jaw should always be loose and hanging from its hinges. The temporal-mandibular joint is the area where the jaw joins the skull. It enables the lower jaw to be extremely flexible in movement. Move the jaw around at intervals. Move it gently to the left and right; create easy circles. The flexibility of the jaw can be related to the pelvis; strong emotions often abide in both areas.

Energizing is also a popular form of relaxation. Energizing is accomplished by tensing each area of the body and then relaxing, starting with the feet and working upwards to areas of the head.

You can alternate draining of energy with energizing by first energizing and then proceeding to the oozing out of physical and mental energies.

Hanging Loose

Loosening, as with breathing, is the most accessible means of relaxing the body and mind. Some people prefer it under certain circumstances when they lack the time to abide by a systematically prescribed procedure.

You loosen by voluntarily shaking off stress, kinks, knots, and tight muscles. Empty yourself of any physical discomfort.

Make expressive dance movements to release tense muscles. Shake like a leaf, stretch or do push-ups. Go through an aerobic dance routine.

Zero in on the neck, the area of common stress. Let your

head go back; roll it around and do neck circles 10 to 15 times.

Squeeze the eyes and then relax them. Move the jaw left and right, up and down. Alternately energize (make faces) and relax the facial muscles.

Melt like butter and feel your arms hang like spaghetti. Relax the many strings of nerves that cling to muscles.

Feel your head, eyes, lids, jaw, brain and neck become like one big marshmallow.

Sense pent-up energy in the body draining through imaginary valves at the tips of the fingers and toes. Let the fingers drip loosely from the knuckles.

What areas of tightness have you discovered? Loosen the tight areas by moving them. When you feel a tense area relaxing, get a feeling of the relaxation spreading through the body.

Let out explosive sounds as you move hinges and sockets in the arms, shoulders, hips and legs.

Breathe and direct oxygen through the bronchial tubes as you expand the lungs. Empty the lungs abruptly.

Direct oxygen into your diaphragm—the partition between chest and abdomen. Expel air with your diaphragm muscles as you blow it out of the mouth.

Sitting Down

Gradually lower yourself into a chair, maintaining the relaxation of mental areas. Melt into the chair as you slump down with legs spread out in a comfortable position, heels resting on the floor. Try not to be concerned about sitting on the edge of the chair and being about to slip off. Let the arms hang loose. Go into a corpse position. Shut out all external sounds. Return and listen to the sounds of your body—arterial sounds, pulsations, stomach gurgles, heartbeat, head noises and breathing.

Try not to assume the same position in the chair each time you do the exercise. A position that is relaxing on one occasion may not be the most relaxing for another. Move around in the chair until you find a comfortable position. Sometimes having the right or left leg stretched out can be more comfortable than stretching both legs. When making adjustments, use only the muscles in the area you are adjusting, e.g., if you wish to move the legs into a more comfortable position, keep the rest of the body relaxed and motionless. You do not need to tighten the jaw muscles or let the upper body go forward in order to adjust the muscles of the legs; this principle also applies to adjusting the arms or other body parts.

Avoid holding on to the sides of the chair and let the arms dangle loosely or have one or both hands rest on your thighs.

If you find an area which is tense, simply give yourself a pleasant command to relax that area. Avoid shaking out tension by moving your arms, legs or neck. Permit the wonderful capacity of the brain to relax tense areas. During performance, if you feel tension creeping into the shoulders or legs, you cannot stop a scene and shake out the tension. But by training the capacity of the mind to send messages to tense areas, you develop the ability to relax while performing. There are always moments in a scene when you can check for tensions. In sending a message to different areas of the body and hidden places, feel the message travel soothingly along the nerve circuitry.

As you slump down in the chair, feel the floor upon which all the weight of the legs bears down—as if your legs and feet are on a scale. Permit the chair to absorb all of your weight, tensions, and muscular feelings.

If your fingers tend to wiggle and move (a common happening in daily life), discover the nerve routes up the arms, across the shoulders, including the back of the neck. The fingers (and toes) are connected to nerve routes and that is why both hands and feet can simultaneously have excessive little movements. Relax the nerve routes and the wiggling movements will diminish considerably.

Tension in a forefinger is not tension in a small and insignificant area, but can easily involve a whole group of muscles. Tension in the right forefinger, for example, may have begun somewhere on the left side of the body and traveled over a whole group of muscles before manifesting itself in the right forefinger.

Keep the fingers limp and not turned inwards. Fingers which are turned inwards may be caused by the way your cartilage is formed, but it is for you to discover whether this is so or not. Tension in the hands, particularly the fingers, is frequently overlooked.

The head need not be in a straight upward position, but can droop forward with the chin resting on the chest; or the head can hang to one side or the other.

Pause a while as you explore outer and inner areas during your physical relaxation and let the head go back gently. When you let the head hang back, it may at first be uncomfortable, but in time you will discover it can hang back for any length of time. Be sure that you keep the mental areas relaxed as the head goes back and returns to a forward position. The forward position can be one in which the head alternately hangs to the sides. If you feel the mental areas become more relaxed as the head moves forward, it may mean that there has been some holding on in the neck.

If there is any problem in getting a general mental relaxation while working specifically on the physical, you can alternate the two. For example, specifically relax the legs, but before moving to another physical area, check the relaxation of the mental areas. The ultimate aim of the exercise, however, is to simultaneously relax other areas on a moment's notice—an ever-present demand from audition to performance.

Breathing

Following are a number of choices for breathing and you may wish to try them all.

Just sitting and breathing can be totally relaxing; it can be done for a few minutes or as long as 15 minutes.

Feel the oxygen enter your nose, moving into the nostrils and passing through the nose hairs as it subsequently moves down into parts of the body. Holistic practitioners advise you to breathe deeply through the nose and feel it go to your center which is slightly below the navel.

Establish an even rhythm as you breathe in relaxation. Let your mind and body go with the exhalation as you breathe out tensions and harmful carbon dioxides.

Establish a breathing rhythm by inhaling on a count of six, hold for a count of three and exhale on a count of six. The count can change from one occasion to another, and you may wish to formulate the count to suit the moment. Repeat the cycle as often as you wish.

Are you exhaling interfering or unwanted thoughts? Give in to their expiration. Breathe deep into the body, all the way down to the balls of the feet. Some Yogis breathe slowly through the mouth and exhale slowly through the nose.

Are there constrictions in the neck area adjoining the top of the spine? Are there constrictions in such areas as the stomach or pelvis? Breathe into and exhale from those areas. Visualize the life-giving force of oxygen going into all the organs of the body. Some suggest letting the air go out through the buttocks instead of the nostrils.

You can direct oxygen to areas of pain and discomfort. Permit the oxygen to purify such areas and then exhale the impurities and contaminants through a relaxed jaw and mouth. Not all oxygen goes to the lungs; 35% of it goes to the brain and you can direct inhalation to cleanse affected areas. Direct the oxygen to a pain and imagine the exhalation actually going through the flesh and skin covering the pain area.

Esoteric breathing images have been beneficial for many people. Breathe the sun into the whole body and breathe out moon energy. Surround yourself with golden light and breathe it in.

Testing Mental Areas

Let all mental areas melt: the temples, brow, bridge of nose, eyelids, eyeballs, optic nerves, the temple-nerves at the side of the eyes; loosen the scalp; feel energy dripping out of the cheeks; let the jaw hang loosely with teeth and lips comfortably separated. Relax the jaw hinges through which pass most of the nerve circuits from the brain which send messages to the body. Loosen any holding on in the jaw hinges.

Relax the face so that deep interior qualities can surface and be seen in relaxed facial muscles. Long-distance runners have discovered that they waste calories by tightening the muscles of the face. By relaxing the face, they put the calories to use to help them run faster. During a peak emotion in acting, a relaxed face will permit the dynamics of an inner emotion to create more interesting facial nuances.

Refrain from blinking. Let the eyelids open slightly and heavily. Close the partially open lids as if they were weights sinking slowly into water. Repeat this a few times. Let the lids come together gently. The partial, sleepy-like opening and closing of the lids should be done at several intervals during the physical relaxation.

As you maintain the relaxation of the mental areas, gently let the head go back. As the head goes back, feel the tiny vertebrae in the neck. Let the head hang back for a while as you sense a general releasing of the nerves throughout the body beginning from the ganglia of nerves in the back of the neck.

Bring the head forward and let it droop to the side or hang forward. Do neck circles.

Deeper Physical Relaxation

Although many disciplines attempt to shut out any distracting sound, some people are unable to accomplish this in all circumstances. In that event, find a way of using sound as a focus. A student in my workshop had great difficulty with mental relaxation at the beginning of the

relaxation period. After many months, he heard a cat me-
owing in an adjoining church garden, and by going with the
sound, he was able to relax more quickly. I suggested that
he choose a sensory stimulus at the beginning of his relaxation by creating an inner sanctuary of sounds and smells of
the sea, a meadow, a forest or other locales. He was to
continue this process until he felt he could mentally relax
more quickly, knowing that he could always return to sensory stimuli when difficulties recurred. Since the performer
works under many types of trying circumstances, this example demonstrates that you can always find a solution in
the balance between yourself and your professional surroundings.

In your sitting position, feel the stretching taking place
in your body. Relax the large muscle groups in the arms
and legs, including the hands and feet. Sequentially, begin
to relax other areas, particularly the hidden areas in the
armpits, back of the neck and the small of the back. Investigate the pelvic area in which there can be a lot of holding
on, particularly in the genitalia and anus areas.

Now you are ready to journey into the body as your
conscious thoughts pass through and monitor the recesses
of tissues, muscles, flesh, fibers, tendons, etc. You are now
permitting your body and mind to collaborate. Although
you will be sending forth commands from the mind to relax
discovered body tensions, try not to regard those commands as strict and authoritative, but part of pleasant discoveries.

The journey into the body should be a fresh experience
each time you do the exercise. Rid yourself of muscular
battles and calmly be your own monitor as you get into the
organs, flesh and muscles which surround the bones. Sense

the flesh and the beautiful latticework within it. Some people relax right down to their bones.

Finding Your Center

When you are physically relaxed, you are ready to begin the mental relaxation. During the physical part of the exercise, you partially relaxed mental areas and now are prepared to work on them more specifically.

Give yourself a final check while still slumped down in the chair. Are you still physically relaxed in all areas? Tension moves around and a tension you may have eliminated in one area may have moved into another area.

Gradually draw the legs towards you until the feet are comfortably apart (about 10 or 12 inches) and pointing forward. Let the legs design a right-angle position with a straight line going out from the hips to the knees down through the ankles. The space between the knees and ankles should be equal and the thighs and calves in a parallel position. The toes and knees should point directly ahead. Sense an energy proceeding in a forward direction from all these areas.

As you move from the physical position into an aligned position for the mental, you may find it helpful to first visualize your body in alignment before executing the necessary movements. Visualize a comfortable alignment, rather than any kind of position that requires effort.

Without thrusting the upper part of the body forward (including the head/neck area), gently move into a sitting position, pressing lightly against the floor with the balls of your feet to give you a little leverage. At the same time, begin to align the head, neck and spine. When you have completed the movement, the upper and lower body should be aligned. Keep the jaw relaxed and eyelids heavy as you do the movement. After the movement is completed, check for relaxation in the buttocks, small of the back and leg muscles—all of which were used to make the movement.

You should not think of the aligned position as rigid or overly postural, but one that is comfortable and centered. Feel energy traveling up and down the spine and from the small neck vertebrae into the head.

Permit the head to sit easily on the neck without any leaning forward, backward or to the sides. Make adjustments by contacting the swivel bone in the neck. Often a proper alignment of the head and neck can be accomplished by having a sense of moving only the top of the head to the left or right until it is centered. Effective alignment can also be attained by moving only the chin to the left or right. Observe these adjustments in a mirror.

Finding your center is an artistic responsibility; it is creating your own circle. In this exercise, you are only asked to keep the body aligned for a short period of time. Yogis and Swamis do it for up to nine hours.

The alignment position may seem uncomfortable in the beginning, but will not remain so. It is optional whether or not your back touches the back of the chair. In Zen meditation, sitting in a chair is the easiest of five meditation positions. It is based on the ancient Egyptian method of meditational sitting. You may eventually have the feeling that you are not sitting on a chair at all, but that your body is floating. Permit the chair to accept the weight of your body as you maintain a comfortable alignment. Find your own center in the way you would find the center (or off-center) of a character—a prim character will have a tight center, while a lopsided type will have an asymmetrical center. Notice the comfortable center of some notable people during interview talk shows on television.

Feel an energy flow in your alignment—from the base of the spine up to the head and back down the spine again. Maintaining alignment is greatly helped if you think of the neck as a bridge between the body and the head, rather than letting it be an improper barrier. Even people who have had a broken back, or have a spinal problem, are able to find ways of giving a semblance of alignment.

When you are in an aligned position, sense how the inner organs are not pressing against one another as they may have been in the slumped down physical position. Contact the smooth flow not only in the organs but throughout the body.

Learn how to introduce a more harmonious center to your daily activities. Sometimes, balance and peace can be rare in our private lives. We know we have the capacity to attain it, but often lack the patience and neglect to take the necessary time.

Deeper Mental Relaxation

Mental relaxation is more important than physical relaxation, but for many it is not easily attainable. Physical tension is more observable than mental tension. Mental tension is observable in a tense face, wrinkled brow or tight lips. However, even without these facial mannerisms, mental tension can still function almost invisibly, deep within mental areas.

Begin to be aware of any thoughts and permit them to float away. Become detached from them. You cannot always stop your thoughts, even with effort, but you can let them disappear into the space around you. Try not to be an audience for your thoughts. Let them find an audience elsewhere. When you control the thinking process and mentally relax, you are relaxing the left brain where more chattering goes on than in the right brain.

These are the areas to further relax: the temples, the brow (including the scalp and the bridge of the nose), the entire eye area (lids, eyeballs and optic nerves), and areas of the cheeks, mouth and jaw. Particular emphasis is placed on the jaw as tension here may mirror a deeper tension elsewhere in the body's organs and muscles. Some people feel less stomach discomfort when they learn how to relax a tight jaw.

The first mental area relates to the overloaded circuitry of the temples, with its network of blue nerves and blood vessels which feed into the brain. The temples are not just at the side of the head but extend to the side of the eyes. The temple nerves actually enter into the eyelids. Visualize the temples as being in knots and unravel them; let them be as loose as jelly as you control the flow of blood in the temple areas. Preferably, keep the lids gently closed until it is time to work with the eye area.

Glide into the forehead area. Let the brow and bridge of the nose melt. As the forehead melts, sense the entire scalp loosening. The forehead muscles are important since they are directly related to the relaxation of scalp, neck and upper part of the body. Check for any tension across the top of the eyebrows. Feel a gentle flow between the skin layers of the scalp and the skull. Sense the flow all the way to the back of the head. Sometimes there can be a low awareness of the tightness that exists at the back of the head. As with all mental areas, feel a calm radiating all over the scalp area.

Mental relaxation is not only free self-analysis but also a free facial treatment as wrinkles and lines caused by tension begin to dissolve.

Gradually move into the areas of the eyes. First melt the muscles around the eyes. Let the lids be gently together or have a very slight opening so that only a slit of light enters. Relax the optic nerve tracts that meet inside the back of the head and then move into the brain's two hemispheres. This is why the optic nerves and brain are really the same organ. The optic nerves are actually extensions of the brain.

Eighty percent of the information we receive is through the eyes, which accounts for the eye area being a source of tension. Not only are the eyes the chief source of information, but they also report our state of mind. They use up a lot of energy during daily activities and our whole being is affected when that energy creates a tense state.

Let the energy in the eyelids melt and ooze down the side of the nose onto the cheeks. Make sure that both the eyeballs and eyelids are relaxed. Sometimes the eyelids may be relaxed but the eyeballs are not, or vice versa.

Begin to open the lids with one-quarter or one-third openings. Sense their heaviness as you open them slightly and feel them sinking when you close them. It is advisable to start with small openings. The muscles which open and close the lids may need to be retrained in order to get smooth, heavy, uninterrupted openings and closings. This retraining is often necessary to prepare you for half-way openings and closings. The final goal in this process is, of course, full opening and closing with heavy, relaxed lids.

The movement of the lids should be an uninterrupted gliding movement with no staircase stops and flutterings.

When the lids close, feel them sink like a weight in water as they skim lightly downward over the eyeballs. When you open the eyes all the way, be aware of any tendency to blink rapidly. If sudden blinking occurs, gently hold the lids open, contact the blinking muscles and get them under control and then let the lids sink heavily. There may be burning in the eyes when you first work with them, even tears, but that will disappear with time and patience. If you wear contact lenses, you can train the lids so the lenses need not be an interference.

Sense the eyeballs floating in the vitreous fluid that surrounds them.

In a workshop setting, look at the environment in a relaxing way without any blinking at lights, moving objects or people. Take only a nominal interest in them. You may even want to softly focus on an object and shut out all others. Calmly blink as you focus on the object in order to avoid staring at it.

Feel the relaxation of the eyelids, eyeballs and the brow move gently into the head area—from the front of the brain to the back of the brain.

The heaviness in half-open eyelids is one that occurs in a meditator's alpha state, or in biofeedback. The alpha state, as you know, permits deep creative intuitions to surface.

Relaxation of the eyes cannot be overemphasized for the film actor, as many film nuances occur with the eyes. The more the film actor is able to relax the eyes, the greater will be the range of nuances.

The next area, the cheeks, has more muscles than any part of the face. This is why emotion often registers strongly in the cheeks. The cheeks also indicate our state of health, just as the eyes can reveal our state of mind. Let the muscles and nerve endings of the cheeks melt away.

A Beverly Hills beauty salon has experimented with biofeedback instruments to relax areas of the face in order to prevent wrinkles that result from tense facial mannerisms. The art of relaxing the tiny facial muscles is your own natural biofeedback and far less costly than salon treatments. Constant tension in the forehead or muscles around the mouth can cause permanent lines and wrinkles. This may also give you some insight as to how our inner organs are marked during prolonged states of stress.

The jaw and mouth are the final areas. In life we are always ready to form words and the speech mechanisms are always active, even in a nonverbal state. The mouth itself is a very active area not only for speech but also for the fulfillment of other daily needs, mostly pleasurable. The tongue is an exceptionally strong muscle and should be relaxed just as any other body muscle. Feel all the energy drain from the mouth, lips, tongue and jaw. Having the jaw relaxed does not mean you have to be a mouth breather during the exercise nor should you be concerned if you look somewhat asthmatic.

The strength of the jaw is known by anthropologists who have discovered several human jaw fossils that date back as much as five million years. It is conclusive proof that it is our strongest skeletal area. In three notable anthropological findings since 1974, the remainder of the bodies belonging to jaw fossils had become dust. We might say that the relaxation exercise concludes with attention to one of our strongest and most enduring areas.

As with meditation, relaxation is a purifying experience enabling transformations. Both meditation and relaxation teach one how to tap hidden energies. When there has been complete faith in developing powers of relaxation, you discover that only a few minutes are needed to reach a state where you are receiving the creative blessings of hidden energies.

Action Choices

To Admire the World
To Admit Past Mistakes
To Advise
To Annihilate the Tyrants
To Argue the Point
To Arrive at the Last Stop
To Assault
To Assert Myself
To Attack
To Attract and Possess All I Desire
To Avoid
To Avoid Being Tracked Down
To Avoid Conversation
To Avoid Delicate Matters
To Avoid Doing the Inevitable
To Avoid the Issue

To Avoid the Truth
To Awaken

To Bait
To Be a Loaded Gun
To Be Connected
To Be Free as a Bird
To Be in Harmony
To Be In Over My Head
To Be On Guard Against
To Beat Down
To Blast
To Bluff My Way
To Bolster Up
To Bomb Them with My Power
To Break Loose
To Break My Back
To Break Out of My Shell

To Break the Balance
To Bring Out the Corrupt
  Nature
To Bring Them to Their
  Knees
To Bruise
To Brush Over Delicate
  Matters
To Burn All My Bridges
To Burst Forward
To Bury My Problems

To Call the Next Move
To Captivate
To Captivate People
To Captivate Their
  Imagination
To Capture
To Carry Out an Important
  Mission
To Cast Off Mediocrity
To Cast Off the Yoke
To Cast Out the Devil
To Catch the Eye
To Change Directions
To Change the Mood
To Change Their Minds
To Chew Up and Spit Out
To Claim My Position
To Climb Out of Myself
To Cling
To Cool Things Off

To Come into My Own
To Come Out on Top
To Complain
To Complain Like Hell
To Complete an Important
  Mission
To Con Everyone
To Confuse Everything
To Connect Everything
To Connect to My Dream
To Connect with the World
To Conquer Evil
To Contain My Moments
To Control People
To Cover Up My Guilt
To Cut the Crap
To Cut Through the Fog

To Defend What Is Mine
To Delve into My Fantasies
To Demand Recognition
To Demand Their Best
To Derail
To Destroy
To Devastate My
  Surroundings
To Devour
To Dictate the Law
To Discover a New Way
To Dive into the Wreck
To Discover the Humor of
  It

To Discover the Truth
To Do My Work
To Do the Inevitable
To Do What I Have to Do
To Dominate Everything
To Draw from the Roots
To Draw the Line
To Dump On

To Encourage Everyone to
  Love the World
To Enforce My Will
To Enlighten
To Escape into Another
  World
To Evade the Issue
To Examine My Folly
To Excite Someone
To Explain Where I'm
  Coming From
To Explore in Detail
To Expose the S.O.B.
To Express My Needs

To Face Up To
To Fight Back
To Fight for What I Believe
  In
To Fight the Lie
To Figure Out
To Find a Place for Myself
To Find Magic

To Find My Bearings
To Find Out
To Find Protection
To Find Something to Do
To Find the Answer
To Find the Dividing Line
To Find the Father in Me
To Find the Mother in Me
To Find the Truth
To Fit In
To Flow with the Tide
To Flush Them Out
To Fly into the Wind
To Fly the Coop
To Follow
To Follow My Star
To Force Connection
To Form a Bond with Those
  About Me
To Free Myself
To Freeze the Blood

To Get All I Can
To Get Along
To Get Away from People
To Get Back on Course
To Get Back to a Better
  Time
To Get in Bed
To Get in Everywhere
To Get It All Out
To Get Next To

To Get Off the Hot Seat
To Get On the Good Side
To Get Out of Myself
To Get Rid of Someone
To Get Some Food
To Get the Job Done
To Get the Upper Hand
To Get Their Attention
To Get Them Off My Back
To Get Things in Focus
To Get to the Heart of the
  Matter
To Get to the Point
To Get Under Their Skin
To Give All the Love I Have
To Give My Power Away
To Give Myself
To Go Against the Grain
To Go All the Way
To Go Back in Time
To Go For It
To Go Off into My Own
  World
To Go One Step Further
To Go Where No Man Has
  Gone Before
To Go with the Flow
To Grope for Words
To Grope in the Dark
To Gross Them Out
To Guide

To Harbor a Grudge
To Haul Over the Coals
To Heal
To Hear the Results
To Hit the Bull's Eye
To Hold Fast to Tradition
To Hold Myself Together
To Hold On to Someone
To Hold On to My Bearings
To Hold Their Interest
To Hold Up
To Hustle a Fast One

To Incite
To Include Another
To Induce
To Inflame
To Inflame Your Brain
To Instigate
To Intimidate
To Investigate
To Invite
To Involve Them in My
  Experience

To Joke with Them
To Jump at the Chance
To Jump In

To Keep a Safe Distance
To Keep an Open Mind
To Keep Everything

To Keep from Ripping Out
Their Guts
To Keep from Being
Destroyed
To Keep from Sinking
To Keep Going
To Keep Going for the Love
of It
To Keep in Touch with
People
To Keep Myself Attached to
People
To Keep the Lid On
To Keep the Situation in
Hand
To Keep Things Going My
Way
To Know When Enough Is
Enough

To Lay My Ass on the Line
To Lead by the Nose
To Lead into a Trap
To Leap the Bull
To Learn How to Connect
To Leave My Old Self
Behind
To Lend Myself to the
Situation
To Let It Out
To Level
To Liberate the Oppressed

To Lift Their Spirits
To Listen
To Live It Up
To Live Moment to
Moment
To Look into Someone's
Soul
To Look on the Bright Side
of Life
To Look Out for Number
One

To Maintain My Balance
To Make Bold My Point of
View
To Make People Do What I
Want Them to Do
To Make a Place for Myself
To Make a Simple
Connection
To Make a Sleazy Deal
To Make a Stand
To Make the Atmosphere
Crackle
To Make the Day Mine
To Make Them
Acknowledge My
Presence
To Make Them Hunger for
More
To Make Them See It My
Way

To Make Them Sorry They
Were Ever Born
To Make Them Understand
To Make Things
Comfortable
To Map Uncharted
Territory
To Master the Possibilities
To Meet My God's
Vengeance
To Mock Everyone
To Mold
To Move from the Center

To Nail
To Needle
To Not Give Up
To Nurture Those Around
Me

To Observe Everything
To Own This Place

To Pay Them Back
To Pester
To Pick Up the Pieces
To Pierce the Universe
To Piss Them Off
To Plant a Seed of Doubt
To Plead My Case
To Please

To Plow Through the
Blizzard
To Possess Everything
To Practice Like a Child
To Prepare Myself for love
To Prepare to Pounce
To Prevail
To Probe
To Protect a Friend
To Protect Myself
To Provoke
To Pry Some Confidential
Information
To Pull Strings
To Pursue an Attraction
To Push My Case
To Push Their Buttons
To Put a Jewel in Your
Crown
To Put Them on the Spot
To Put on Ice
To Put the World in Order
To Put to Proof

To Quell Their Anxiety
To Question Everything
To Quiet

To Ram It Home
Unflinchingly
To Reach My Center
To Realize a Dream

To Realize the Buddha in
Myself
To Rebel Against
To Refuse
To Relish the Moment
To Regain My Confidence
To Remind
To Remove Myself from the
Situation
To Resist
To Respond
To Respond to the Call of
Life
To Retain a Sense of Myself
To Reveal Myself
To Rip Somebody's Guts
Out
To Rouse
To Rule with Power
To Rule the Roost

To Save My Soul
To Save Myself
To Save the World
To Scar
To Seduce
To See All Viewpoints
To See It Through to the
End
To See Nowhere to Go
To See the Horror

To See the World Through
a Child's Eyes
To See Through the Fog
To Seek Comfort
To Seek Greener Pastures
To Seek Hidden Treasure
To Seek Romance
To Seize an Opportunity
To Sell a Bill of Goods
To Sell Crap
To Send Them to Hell
To Set on Fire
To Settle in a Dream
To Shape
To Share My Space
To Show My True Colors
To Show Who's the Boss
To Shut Out the World
To Shut Out the Nightmare
To Skirt the Issue
To Smash
To Sneak Through the Back
Door
To Soak Up Everything
To Solve a Problem
To Spew Philosophic
Rhetoric
To Spin My Web
To Spiritually Lead
To Spoil the Party
To Spring the Trap
To Squirm Through

To Stab
To Stand My Ground
To State My Intentions
To Stay Where I Am
To Stir
To Stir Up the Moment
To Stop This
To Straighten Them Out
To Swim Against

To Take a Chance
To Take Care Of
To Take Charge of Today
To Take in Hand
To Tantalize
To Tear Back to the Raw
  Elements

To Tell It Like It Is
To Tell the Whole Truth
To Think Big
To Throw Off the Rails
To Tower Over
To Trap My Prey
To Try to Do Something
To Try to Find and Answer
To Try to Hit the Target

To Undermine
To Urge

To Wait It Out
To Weaken the Defenses
To Win at Any Cost
To Win Someone Over

Transpersonal Combinations

To discover the truth
Ch. Imp. — Sharp pain in forefinger to buttocks
Sp. Obj. — Glowing miniature angels

To set on fire
Ch. Imp. — Sexual feeling in eyes to hands
Sp. Obj. — Big swarm of honey bees

To chew them up and spit them out
Ch. Imp. — Rage. Whirlpools in feet to eyes and mouth
Sp. Obj. — Pinching fingers

To instigate
Ch. Imp. — Tension in chest to hands
Sp. Obj. — Caressing hands

To be in two different worlds
Ch. Imp. —Sexual excitement from brain to mouth and
body
Sp. Obj. — Beautiful large raindrops

To smash
Ch. Imp. — Flippancy. Genitals to jaw
Sp. Obj. — Spiderwebs

To demolish
Ch. Imp. — Bile from stomach to throat
Sp. Obj. — Festered demons

To free inhibitions
Ch. Imp. — Manna from top of head to hands and bottom
            of feet
Sp. Obj. — Good spirits

To spoil the party
Ch. Imp. — Impatience. Itch in chest to groin
Sp. Obj. — Tarantulas

To tear back to the raw elements
Ch. Imp. — Disgust. Tightness in stomach to cheek bones
Sp. Obj. — Person duplicated

To tease
Ch. Imp. — Fine Chardonnay from genitals to head
Sp. Obj. — Finches

To fight the lie
Ch. Imp. — Nervousness in stomach to feet
Sp. Obj. — Parts of various friends

To tell it like it is
Introjection
Ch. Imp. — Sexual. From eyes to groin

To stand my ground
Introjection
Sp. Obj. — Globs of jello

To be centered
Introjection
Ch. Imp. — Sensitivity from thighs to face
Sp. Obj. — Spotlights on face

To burn leaves
Introjection
Ch. Imp. — Bravery. Vibration in jaw to arms
Sp. Obj. — Burning leaves

To maintain my dignity
PSO — Pine tree
Repeated image of a person

To rebel
Aura — Red
Stimuli — Explosive feeling in chest

To get out of myself
Aura — Red
Personal Object — Inanimate
Pain — Nape of neck

To play with them
IMO — Ice cube
Aura — Green of spleen
Place — Tactile elements

To go back in time
Ch. Imp. — Sexual longing. Warmth of alcohol in
                                 abdomen into entire body
As if I was expecting the worst.

To demand
Aura — Purple
Inner Monologue
Stimuli — Explosive feeling in head

To be on edge
Sp. Obj. — Silk scarves
P&P — Heart to fear its own strength
Aura — Black tongue

To give my power away
Ch. Imp. — Twilight in abdomen to top of head
P&P — Feet to root in fertile earth
OSO — Cheeks

To awaken
P&P — Heart to summon the four winds
Winter cold — Hands, underarms and scalp
Sunshine — Rest of body

To find the truth
P&P — Heart to summon the four winds
Cold — Wrists, ankles and scalp
OSO — Third eye

To celebrate
IMO — Chameleon
Overall — Cool soapy water

To break loose
Ch. Imp. — Tumultuous. Voice in both ears to spine
OSO — Base of spine — hands — eyes

To mock
Aura — Silver — Head
        Red — Rest of body
Sp. Obj. — Gnats and fleas

To raise hell
Ch. Imp. — Restlessness. Chill in base of spine to ears
Personal Object — Animate

To make the atmosphere crackle
Ch. Imp. — Confidence. Pacific Ocean air in head to knees
P&P — Spleen to laugh
As if I were tired enough not to care.

To reproach
Aura — Gold — Reproductive organs
P&P — Hands to stroke the ego
Aura — Red — Heart
P&P — Eyes to pierce
Animal trait — Neck of swan

To hide
Ch. Imp. — Self-conscious. Adrenalin in stomach to face
OSO — Hair — pelvis — tongue
Personal Object

To reveal
PSO — Pistol
Stimuli — Steady beating heart
As if my chest cavity is an open chamber.
Sound — Whispering and crying voices

To be calm under fire
Ch. Imp. — Upset stomach to eyes
IMO — Sharp object

To know my power
IMO — The sun
Sp. Obj. — Jet fighters

To probe the mystery
PSO — Smoky crystal
IMO — Radiating diamond in the chest
Overall — Warm tropical humidity

To inspire
PSO — Live electrical wire
2 IMO — Miniature vibrator in arms and hands
            Pure white flame of truth in torso cavity
Overall — Hot wind

To rise above my anger
IMO — Smoldering volcano in the brain
Sound — Fingernails on blackboard
Overall — Warm fluid
Wandering Personal Object — Massaging hands on back &
                                    shoulders

To explain my circumstance
Sp. Obj. — Hot dogs
Aura — Violet
Animal trait — Essence of cat for arm movements

To capture the moment
Ch. Imp. — Tickle in feet to head
IMO — Sharp object

To break through
P&P — Thighs for strength
      Genitals for desire
      Hands and feet for reaching out and breaking
      through
OSO — Teeth — jaw

To tease
IMO — Sparkler in brain
Ch. Imp. — Laughter in shoulders into body
OSO — Bottom lip

To make bold my point of view
IMO — Steel ball of varying temperatures
Sp. Obj. — Parts of people

To get lost in my sexual fantasies
Sp. Obj. — Feathers on face
Sp. Obj. — Snakes up and down body
Aura — Black
Place — Visual

To clearly explain my anger
Introjection
P&P — Respiratory system to annihilate

To keep out of trouble
OSO — Pituitary gland
            Solar plexus
Sound — Breaking wine glasses
As if I were crossing a tree trunk over a stream.

To draw the line
P&P — Eyes to see the future
            Elbows to insure my space
            Lungs to assess my situation
            Feet to move in time
OSO — Hands
Aura — Blue

To care
Aura —Gold — Heart
            Blue — Throat
            Red — Waist
Wandering Personal Object — Localized on thighs
Sunshine — Localized on face

To keep attached to people
Ch. Imp. — Electric bursts from pineal gland into legs
IMO — Heavy rocks in both legs
Sp. Obj. — Electromagnetic field
Aura — Red and orange in torso and arms

Section Examples for Scene Work and Monologues

Long Day's Journey into Night by Eugene O'Neill

Given Circumstance
To give up fighting
Sharp pain—Head
Overall—Warm breeze

Sections
1. *To make fun of*
   Sp. Obj— Faces
   Overall—Cold breeze
   Sound—Screaming voices

2. *To cast out the devil*
   Ch. Imp.— Love. Sexual excitement to the face
   Overall—Dry hot wind
   Place—Visual and smell

3. *To awaken*
    Ch. Imp. — Confidence. Electricity in feet to eyes
    Sp. Obj.— Clouds
    Sound—Vivaldi

4. *To let it all out*
    Ch. Imp.— Electricity in stomach to face and into
    veins
    Overall—Hot shower

5. *To face destiny*
    Pain—Heart area
    Place—Visual
    2 Wandering Personal Objects

Painting Churches by Tina Howe

Given Circumstance
To find my bearings
Ch. Imp.— Amber aura from balls of feet to heart and
hands
Inner Monologue
Stimuli—Tingling lips

Sections
1. *To become inspired*
   Ch. Imp.—Same as in Given Circumstance
   Repeated image—Twilight
   Introjection—5th grade teacher

2. *To reckon with the past*
   Ch. Imp.—Same as #1
   2 Repeated images juxtaposed: Twilight
                                    Painting
   Introjection—Same as #1

3. *To struggle to finish it*
   Ch. Imp.—Same
   Repeated image—Painting
   Stimuli—Tingling lips

Loose Ends by Michael Weller

Given Circumstance
To get my bearings
OSO—Nerves from all parts of body
Sp. Obj.—Millions of bubbles
Hot coals on bottom of feet

Sections

1. *To make a simple connection*
   Sp. Obj.—Needles
   IMO—Razor blades in veins

2. *To evade the issue*
   IMO—Waves in head
            Bees in stomach stinging occasionally
   OSO—Heart

3. *To make a stand*
   Ch. Imp.—Itchy eyes to arms and chest
   Brain— Right hemisphere to left side of body:
            Explosions
   Left brain to right side of body: Hot lava

4. *To cut the crap*
   Ch. Imp.—Fingernails being pulled to throat

5. *To ram it home*
   Image— Thousands of bodies being bulldozed
            into large holes
   As if I lost all and am now living on the streets.

G.R.Point by David Berry

Given Circumstance

To cover my guilt
As if I had been running.

Sections

1. *To maintain my dignity*
   Ch. Imp.—Sensation in stomach to eyes
   Place—Lake at dusk
   Sound—Loons

2. *To fight the lie*
   Ch. Imp.— Sensation in eyes to mouth, hands
             and body
   Overall—Cold water

3. *To confront the truth*
   As if I were playing an arcade game.
   Sound—Carnival

4. *To impale*
   Sp. Obj.—Burning meteorites
   Overall—Red ants

5. *To purge*
   Ch. Imp.—Bitter hot oil from stomach to mouth
   Sp. Obj.—Cold hands
   Personal Object

Fool for Love by Sam Shepard

Given Circumstance
To keep from being destroyed
IMO—Clock ticking in head
   Razor blades in veins

Sections

1. *To force connection*
   Ch. Imp.—Fire in feet into head and body
   Sp. Obj.—Needles
   Sound—Sirens and horns honking

2. *To see no where to go*
   Sp. Obj.—Fireballs
   Stimuli—Inability to swallow
   Overall—Cold shower

3. *To make love to her*
   Sharp pain—Lungs
   Extreme heat—Face
   OSO—Sexual parts
   Place—Visual (middle of sea)

4. *To cover up my guilt*
   Ch. Imp.— Warmth from base of spine through
               spinal column and into head
   OSO—Hands and feet

5. *To show who's the boss*
   IMO—Brain of Mozart in stomach
      Fire in the brain

6. *To go off into my own world*
   Sound—Beethoven
   Smell—Fresh grass and flowers
   Wandering Personal Object—Hand shovel

7. *To plead my case*
   IMO—Baby rattle in head
          Cement poles in body
   OSO—Heart and connecting tissues

Loose Ends by Michael Weller

Given Circumstance
To make the day mine
Aura—Deep peacock blue (used throughout scene)

Sections
1. *To be forced to face the music*
    Double Ch. Imp.— Nervous stomach to eyes
                     Tension in arms to entire body

2. *To hear the lunacy of it all*
    IMO—M&M's in torso
    Sp. Obj.—Flyswatters

3. *To let down my guard*
    Aura—Grey
    Place—Visual

4. *To feel the love between them*
    P&P— Eyes to see sincerity
         Heart to pump out charm
         Hands to reach out
    Wandering Personal Object

5. *To express my needs*
    Sp. Obj.—Cat crap
    Overall—Heat from hot stage lights
    Place—Visual

6. *To stall the reality*
    As if this were all a bad movie.

A Moon for the Misbegotten by Eugene O'Neill

Given Circumstance
To win her over and expose her
Place—Feeling of sinking into it

Sections
1. *To play the tune*
   Wandering Personal Object—Feather

2. *To find the truth*
   Sound—Symphonic music

3. *To quiet fear*
   Sp. Obj.—People

4. *To know sexual abandon*
   Aura—Green—Black

5. *To find the answer*
   Highlight— Disbelief: Headache
   Breathless: Pain in chest

6. *To cut the bullshit*
   Ch. Imp.— Anger. Electric current in arms to entire body

7. *To express myself*
   Introjection

Bibliography and Sources

Alexander, Shana: "The Grandfather of all Cool Actors Becomes the Godfather." New York: *Life Magazine*, March 10, 1973. Quotation reprinted by permission of the publisher.

Artaud, Antonin: *The Theatre and Its Double*. New York: Grove Press, 1958.

Assagioli, Roberto: *The Act of Will*. Baltimore: Penguin Books Inc., 1974.

Assagioli, Roberto: *Psychosynthesis*. New York: The Viking Press, 1965.

Atkinson, Brooks: *Broadway*. New York: The MacMillan Co., 1970.

Auribindo, Sri: *The Mind of Light*. New York: E.P. Dutton, 1971.

Benedetti, Jean: *Stanislavski: A Biography*. London: Routledge, 1988.

Bennett, J. G.: *Gurdjieff: Making of a New World*. New York: Harper and Row, 1973.

Boslough, John: *Stephen Hawking's Universe: An Introduction to the Most Remarkable Scientist of Our Time*. New York. Quill/William Morrow, 1985.

Boyd, Doug: *Rolling Thunder*. New York: Dell Publishing Co., 1974.

Boyd, Doug: *Swami*. New York: Random House, 1976.

Campbell, Joseph: *The Power of Myth*. New York: Doubleday, 1988.

Capra, Fritoj: *The Tao of Physics*. New York: Bantam, 1977.

Castaneda, Carlos: *Journey to Ixtlan*. New York: Simon and Schuster, 1972.

Clurman, Harold: *The Fervent Years: The Story of the Group Theatre and the Thirties*. New York: Alfred A. Knopf, 1950.

Chekhov, Michael. *To the Actor*. New York: Harper and Row, 1953.

Cherkasov, N.: *Notes of a Soviet Actor*. Moscow: Foreign Languages Publishing House.

Conze, Edward: *Buddhism: Its Essence and Development*. New York, Harper & Row, 1975.

D'Andrea, Jeanne and West, Stephen, Editors: *The Spiritual in Art: Abstract Painting 1890 – 1985*. Los Angeles: Los Angeles County Museum of Art, 1980.

Deikman, Arthur, J.: *The Observing Self: Mysticism and Psychotherapy*. Boston: Beacon Press, 1982.

Ferguson, Marilyn: *The Acquarian Conspiracy: Personal and Social Transformation in the 1980's*. Los Angeles: J. P. Tarcher, 1980.

Ferguson, Marilyn: *The Brain Revolution: The Frontiers of Mind Research*. New York: Taplinger Publishing Company, 1973. Quotation reprinted by permission of the publisher.

Gorchakov, Nikolai M.: *Stanislavsky Directs*. New York: Grosset & Dunlap, 1954.

Graham, Sheilah: *The Garden of Allah*. New York: Crown Publishers, 1970.

Gruen, J.: "I Cannot Possibly Make Hitler Sympathetic." New York: *The New York Times*, September 10, 1972. Quotation reprinted by permission.

Grof, Stanislav: *The Adventure of Self-Discovery*. Albany: State University of New York Press, 1988.

Grof, Stanislav: *Beyond the Brain: Birth, Death and Transcendence in Psychotherapy*. Albany: State University of New York Press, 1985.

Hawking, Stephen W.: *A Brief History of Time: From the Big Bang to Black Holes*. New York: Bantam, 1988.

Herrigel, Eugen: *The Method of Zen*. New York: Pantheon Books, 1960.

Herrigel, Eugen: *Zen in the Art of Archery*. New York: Pantheon Books, 1953.

Houghton, Norris: *Moscow Rehearsals: The Golden Age of the Soviet Theatre.* New York: Grove Press, 1936.

Houghton, Norris: *Return Engagement: A Postscript to "Moscow Rehearsals."* New York: Holt, Rinehart and Winston, 1962.

Ichazo, Oscar: "Oscar Ichazo and the Arica Institute." (A conversation between Oscar Ichazo and Sam Keen.) *Psychology Today*, July 1973. New York: Ziff Davis Publishing Company. Quotation reprinted by permission of the publisher.

Jaynes, Julian: *The Origin of the Unconscious in the Breakdown of the Bicameral Mind.* Boston: Houghton Mifflin, 1977.

Joy, Brugh, W.: *Joy's Way: A Map for The Transformational Journey.* Los Angeles: J.P. Tarcher, Inc. 1978.

Karlfried, Graf von Durckheim: *Daily Life as Spiritual Exercise.* New York: Harper and Row, 1972.

Kaushik, Dr. R.P.: *The Ultimate Transformation.* Woodstock: Journey Publications, 1977.

Kazan, Elia: *A Life.* New York: Alfred A. Knopf, 1988.

Kurtz, Ron and Prestera, Hector: *The Body Reveals.* New York: Harper and Row, 1976.

Leonard, George: *The Silent Pulse.* New York: Bantam, 1981.

Logan, Joshua: *My Up and Down, In and Out Life.* New York: Delacorte Press, 1976.

Magarshak, David: *Stanislavski: A Biography.* London: Faber and Faber, 1950.

Magarshak, David: *Stanislavski on the Art of the Stage.* New York: Hill and Wang, 1962.

Maslow, Abraham A.: *The Farther Reaches of Human Nature.* New York: Viking Press, 1971.

Maslow, Abraham A: *Motivation and Personality.* New York: Harper & Row, 1954.

Maslow, Abraham A: *Towards a Psychology of Being.* New York: Van Nostrand, Second edition, 1968. Quotation reprinted by permission of the publisher.

Muktananda, Swami: *In the Company of a Siddha.* Oakland: S.Y.D.A. Foundation, 1978.

Matthews, Brander: *Papers on Acting.* New York: Hill and Wang, 1958.

Olivier, Laurence: *Confessions of an Actor.* New York: Penguin Books, 1984.

Olivier, Laurence: *On Acting.* New York: Simon and Schuster, 1986.

Ornstein, Robert: "Right and Left Thinking.": *Psychology Today Magazine*, May, 1973. Ziff-Davis Publishing Co.

Ouseley, S.G.J., *Colour Meditations.* London: L. N. Fowler & Co., Ltd., 1949.

Ouspensky, P. D.: *In Search of the Miraculous.* New York: Harcourt Brace Jovanovich, Inc., 1949.

Progoff, Ira: *Jung, Synchronicity and Human Destiny.* New York: Dell Publishing Co., 1973.

Rudnitsky, Konstantin: *Russian and Soviet Theatre*. Translated by Roxane Permer. New York: Harry N. Abrams, 1989.

Roose-Evans, James: *Experimental Theatre: From Stanislavsky to Today*. New York: Universe Books, 1970.

Schultheis, Rob: *Bone Games: One Man's Search for the Ultimate Athletic High*. New York: Random House, 1984.

Schwarz, Jack: *The Path of Action*. New York: E.P. Dutton, 1977.

Selzer, Milton: *Mortal Lessons: Notes on the Art of Surgery*. New York: Simon & Schuster, 1977.

Speeth, Kathleen Riordan: *The Gurdjieff Work*. New York: Pocket Books, 1976.

Stanislavski, Constantin: *Creating a Role*. New York: Theatre Arts Books, 1961.

Stanislavski, Constantin: *Stanislavski's Legacy*. Edited by Elizabeth Reynolds Hapgood. New York: Theatre Arts Books, 1958.

Stanislavski, Constantin: *My Life in Art*. Boston: Little, Brown & Co., 1924.

Stanislavski, Constantin: *My Life in Art*. Moscow: Foreign Languages Publishing House.

Strasberg, Lee: *A Dream of Passion: The Development of the Method*. Boston: Little, Brown & Co., 1987.

Tairov, Alexander: *Notes of a Director*. Coral Gables, Florida: University of Miami Press, 1969.

Toolan, John: *Facing West From California Shores*. New York: Crossroads, 1987.

Trungpa, Chogyam: *Shambhala: The Sacred Path of the Warrior*. New York: Anchor Press/Doubleday, 1981.

Tulane Drama Review: "Stanislavski and America" 1: Volume 9, Number 1. New Orleans: Tulane Drama Review, 1964.

Tulane Drama Review: "Stanislavski and America" 2: Volume 9, Number 2. New Orleans: Tulane Drama Review, 1964.

Tulku, Tarthang: *Gesture of Balance*. Berkeley: Dharma Publishing, 1977.

van der Post, Laurens: *Jung & The Story of Our Time*. New York: Pantheon Books, 1975.

Vaughan, Frances E.: *Awakening Intuition*. New York: Anchor Press/Doubleday, 1979.

Weisberger, Edward, Editor: *The Spiritual in Art: Abstract Painting 1890–1985*. Los Angeles: Los Angeles County Museum of Art, 1986.

Wilber, Ken: *Up From Eden: A Tranpsersonal View of Human Evolution*. New York: Anchor Press/Doubleday, 1981.

Williams, Jay: *Stage Left*. New York: Charles Scribner's Sons, 1974.